I Felt The Hand Of God

To Paulette
May you be divinely
inspired as you read
[illegible]
Roger Warner's 13
2009.

The author assumes full responsibility for the accuracy of all facts and quotations as cited in this book.

Unless otherwise noted, all Scripture references are from the King James Version.

ISBN: 1-4196-6361-5
ISBN-13: 978-1419663611

Visit www.booksurge.com to order additional copies.

V D MARSHALL

I FELT THE HAND OF GOD

A GRIPPING STORY OF A SHATTERED DREAM

2007

I Felt The Hand Of God

CONTENTS

To

Maria, My Wife And Josiah My Son.

My Adopted Mum And My Adopted Brothers And Sisters.

The Group Of Young People Who Formed Action 2000 With Whom I Worked And Who Supported Me During My Mentorship Tenure.

PROLOGUE

"It's a process that involves accepting the purpose for which God created you, even if it's not the life you envisioned for yourself" (Partow, *Becoming a Vessel God Can Use*, 1996: 20)

Living a life without a purpose is like charting a massive ship on the boisterous, choppy sea without a sail or a navigational chart. We all have a purpose on Earth and in spite of our dreams, we need to be focused in order to fulfil that purpose. If we believe otherwise it is a case of entertaining the post-modern philosophical movement of existentialism that advocates the view that people are the product of their actions as opposed to being guided by intentions and potentialities. Davidson remarks "that the Lord of heaven and earth has given each of us life and a destiny."[1] The aforementioned thought reinforces my view that one's destiny is based on his/her purpose for living to the extent that such intentions will propel an individual to fulfil that purpose, and so reaching the ultimate destiny of living in the new earth and the new heaven.

The path described in the first part of *I Felt the Hand of God* seeks to track my journey towards the realisation that there is more to this present life than earthly pursuits. By reframing our personal experiences and circumstances, we can be guided to our divinely ordained path. Having witnessed my dream being shattered and being emotionally wounded, I recognise the need to be open-minded with God and be honest with myself. Our passion for a particular field and our willingness to excel in our careers tend to cloud our vision of the divine plan for our lives. We are prohibited from seeing the bigger picture. To court a one-track mind causes us to lose ultimate satisfaction and the peace beyond our understanding.

The pain we suffer from our broken dreams and the struggles we undergo are prime examples that "we must go through many hardships to enter the kingdom of God" (Acts 14:21, NIV). Indeed, trials are powerful tools that we should not despise or meddle with in order to curtail the pain they bring. The devastating moments during our journey are a means of moulding and humbling us. The stark reality is that the process cannot be rushed. During our agonizing moments we need to exercise patience as we intercede for a spiritual breakthrough for others and for ourselves.

I Felt the Hand of God helps us to come to terms with the fact that as individuals go through adverse personal issues, two types of people emerge. One individual may be faithful, optimistic, and determined as he/she relies on divine help and is drawn nearer to the Sovereign God. In contrast, another is pessimistic and rigid, allowing the experiences to push him/her away from God. It's the perspective you grasp that contributes to your choice.

If you have been a victim of a shattered dream, if you have been struggling to find your purpose in life, then you can be helped to accept a paradigm shift in your life by reading this book. This book is also for those whose lives have been turned upside down and have no control over the events. There are those who mentor individuals, helping them to find meaning to their lives. *I Felt the Hand of God* is also written with you in mind.

Struggling to fulfil a dream that continuously escapes your grasp doesn't bring peace or relief. It produces pain, grief, sadness, and frustration. It sets us up for suicide and leads us to become pessimistic. In the end, it triggers us to hate ourselves because we think we cannot achieve important stuff. It is my heartfelt belief that the numerous experiences I gained and the variety of lessons learnt while seeking God's purpose for my life should be shared. I promise you that these experiences will be heart-wrenching, challenging and inspiring. I encourage you to reflect on and absorb the insights that this book provides.

Apart from tracking the journey, there is also the need to apply the knowledge that you have accumulated. Here is where the second part of *I Felt the Hand of God* can become practical to your situation. With all the knowledge we possess, it seldom gets used, and even though we quibble that knowledge is power, we are seldom as powerful as we should be because of our inability to engage in the application of the knowledge we have stored up. Being exposed to some of the principles that are described in this inspiring book, you will have a better understanding of how to gain the victory that you need, even when your dream is shattered. By prayerfully reading *I Felt the Hand of God*, you will discover that there is somebody who truly cares about you and who is still involved in miraculously changing lives. May you be motivated to find your purpose in life.

PART ONE
Tracking the Unforgettable Path

1
At The Beginning

"The heavenly universe is waiting for the members to become channels through which the current of life shall flow to the world" (*The Bible Echo,* Aug. 12, 1901, quoted in Christian Service, p. 21)

Many times we believe that the affairs of other people will be looked after, while we are busy with our personal affairs. We express many sentiments such as somebody is already looking after those helpless people or I do not have the skills needed to do that kind of work. Perhaps we do not understand the seriousness of the expressions. As God's created beings, we reach a point in our life when we recognise that marginal involvement in secular activities is insufficient. Inevitably, we reach a stage where we yearn earnestly for something more from Jehovah-Jireh, our provider. Our Earthly achievements profit little in the long run because they only last for a while. No wonder Ellen White notes that after our riches are moth-eaten and decayed from rust, "Christ's followers can rejoice in their heavenly treasure, the riches that are imperishable." [2] It is, therefore, evident that casual involvement requires more of our effort to the point that "everyone who names the name of Christ should so work that others, by seeing His good works, may be led to glorify their Creator and Redeemer."[3]

With a strong desire of this kind, we are driven to our knees in prayer and, at times, are driven to tears because of our desperate plea for the divine in-filling. In citing Jesus' advice to His disciples before He left this world: "Tarry ye in the city of Jerusalem until ye be endued with power from on high" (Luke 24:49), I realise that they were instructed to spend time communing with the Lord. Luke, in recording the events that occurred immediately after Jesus' ascension to Heaven, paints an interesting picture by recording that they went into an upper room (Acts1:13). What were they doing in the 'upper room'? What was going through their minds at that time? Their behaviour indicates that they took Jesus at His word. From all accounts, they were praying earnestly, confessing one to another, and asking for forgiveness, so that they may receive the power of the Holy Spirit.

As I reflect on my Christian experience over the past eighteen years, my involvement in church work varied. I was Personal Ministries Leader for five years, associate elder, head elder, Sabbath school teacher, youth leader and mentor to the new converts. During these times, I have had some very rewarding and challenging times. There are times when I asked the Lord for a new experience, and indeed, He would open the floodgates to the point that some of these experiences almost cost me my life. The critical lesson I glean from all of this is that I should be careful for what I pray. On reflecting, since 1997, I had been seeking, through prayer and human efforts, for a scholarship to pursue post-graduate studies. I had just completed my undergraduate studies in Linguistics and Educational Psychology. There was an inner motivation to pursue my studies further. And I desperately was craving to enter the field of psychology. I would check the notice board of the university at least twice per week for advertisements about scholarships. At times, I spoke with my former lecturers and professors who had prior knowledge about and experience in obtaining scholarships.

During my search, I found six advertisements for scholarships. I was eligible for them. Immediately, I secured the application forms, all of the required documents and quickly despatched them to the appropriate overseas countries. Within two months, I received replies from each application. Each of the awarding organisations told me that the competition was extremely high. I was unsuccessful. The news shattered me immensely because I believed that my chances of being selected for a scholarship were high. My heart sank deeply. Despondency was etched on my face. By this time, there were hardly any advertisements on the notice board and I wasn't aware of any others. My need to achieve academically uncovered the conscientious element of my personality. It is that trait that is driven by self-discipline, dutifulness, and a deliberate attitude. What propelled me to search for a scholarship? Was there an underlying agenda? Was it a means of preparing for a greater task? Such are the unanswered questions that only the passage of time can answer.

In the summer of 1998, I accompanied the West Seventh-day Adventist Church Pathfinders Club on an eight mile hike. Twenty children between the age of six and fifteen went on the trip. Apart from myself and the Pathfinders' leader, there were two other adults helping with the children. It was a cool day, with the early morning sun sliding along our backs. There was the potential for the scorching sun to rain its heat down on energetic walkers. And so, we set off on the much anticipated pedestrian trip very early that Thursday morning to avoid the penalty for starting late. A cool, refreshing breeze escaped from among the large, swaying trees. The Eastern wind bathed our partially perspiring bodies. The early morning heat was still bearable. It was a serene morning, with little traffic travelling along the route that we leisurely cruised along on. While walking, the Pathfinders' leader and I were sharing our thoughts about the need for a scholarship. Both of us were school teachers: I was at a primary school and taught mainly Mathematics, English, Social Studies, Art and Craft and Religious Knowledge. She was at a secondary/high school where she was specialising in Business Studies.

"I would really like to study overseas, but I don't have that kind of money," she blurted out.

"I have been thinking about the same thing too," I replied as I glanced at her.

She continued, "Scholarships are hard to come by. You would have to know someone high up to get one."

"I could do my Master's at the university," I responded.

With this in mind, she quickly blurted out, "You know what? I saw an advertisement in the newspaper yesterday for a National Development Scholarship. But the deadline is tomorrow."

"That's too soon. There is no way that we can meet that deadline. Plus you have to get documents and references," I answered disappointedly.

Our conversation switched between studies, local church related events and family matters. The children were enjoying the trip as they chatted vibrantly and confidently with each other. Almost all of them had taken out their water bottles, drinks and snacks to regain some needed energy. This Pathfinders' leader is very decisive and determined. She has a big ego, but there was no chance of either of us getting an application in on time. What propelled us to chase our dreams, even though a possible opportunity was slowly escaping our clutches?

"We could well forget about this one," she replied in a rather dejected manner.

"I suppose," I mumbled in a terminating fashion.

Eventually, we came to the end of the hike. We ensured that all of the children had transportation. I went my way and so did she. As I sat in the bus on my way home, I felt the urge to obtain the necessary forms and apply for the scholarship. I immediately jumped for the challenge.

Why don't I go for the forms and fill them out? I thought to myself.

Time was slipping away rapidly from me. If I was going to secure my chance of obtaining a scholarship, I would have to act swiftly. Twenty four hours were left to complete the application form, but in reality, I only had ten business hours to acquire all of the documents.

I wondered, *could I beat the clock?*

The bus was speeding hurriedly along the road, while the Eastern breeze flowed swiftly through the partially opened bus windows. There was a lot of laughter among groups of passengers. I slumped in a relaxed manner in the back seat of the fast-travelling bus. Having arrived at home, I quickly got dressed, telephoned the principal, informed her of my plans and requested a reference from her. Barely putting down the receiver, I scampered out of the house like a racing horse leaving the paddocks on a racing day. I rushed to the scholarship department at the Ministry of Education, and asked for the forms. To my request, the officer in charge queried, "Which scholarship are you applying for?"

A bit uncertain, I replied, "The National Development Scholarship."

He sauntered over to a white shelf littered with numerous other forms, flipped through a pile and then said, "You can have the forms, but the deadline is four o'clock tomorrow. No later."

"I will try to make it back by then," I calmly responded.

"It's up to you."

"Thank you," I said.

As I was leaving, he yelled, "Make sure you bring all the documents that are needed and make sure that your principal signs it."

"Ok."

I carefully perused the application form as I was walking. Having satisfied myself, I quickly set out to travel to the principal's residence to leave the reference section of the application form.

It was Friday. The deadline was four o'clock. I examined the list of documents that were needed, and set about to get them. I felt pressured, but I persevered. I had to obtain passport size photos and photocopies of my qualifications and birth certificate. Along with these documents, I needed a Justice of the Peace to provide an official reference for me and two sureties. I rushed frantically from place to place: in the city centre to get the photographs, to the university to get cheap photocopies, to a colleague's home for the official signature, to the principal's residence for the reference and finally, to the scholarship department. It was a hectic day. With a few minutes left before the deadline, I managed to submit the completed forms on time.

One month later, while at school, I received a telephone call from an official at the Ministry of Education inviting me for an interview in relation to the scholarship. I shared the news excitedly with my colleagues the same time. I could not withhold it. I was delighted to have been considered.

"That was some one from the Ministry of Education. I have to attend an interview tomorrow," I said smiling reservedly.

"Go Marsh," Cindy shouted as she hugged me.

"Do your best," Penelope replied smiling heartily and brightly.

My principal, after waiting her turn, replied convincingly, "I know you will get it. Put your best foot forward."

Having reached the conference room for the interview, to my amazement, I was greeted by ten other colleagues with whom I was well acquainted. We greeted each other as we smiled. Each of us had been invited for the interview. I became aware then that ten scholarships are usually awarded annually to various individuals from different areas of work. We continued to converse, while others were called into the room one at a time. The interview seemed long. In fact, each person spent approximately half of an hour in the room. Some exited the room smiling. Others had sad expressions on their faces. Still others were shaking their heads as if to indicate that they had no chance. It was my turn. I thought I would be nervous. But on the contrary, I was bold, positive and purposeful. I felt well prepared for the barrage of questions.

As I sat, the chairperson confirmed with the other members of the interview panel that I was the new candidate and verified that they had the appropriate documentation. The chairperson checked my name and the primary school at which I was teaching. She quickly introduced her team and herself to me. Then the grilling started. Various members of the panel questioned me about my undergraduate studies. They wanted to know how I was applying the knowledge to the classroom setting.

"What are some of the ways you use your knowledge of Linguistics?" one female interviewer asked firmly.

With my hands resting on my attaché case, I said, "I seek to assist the children in acquiring reading skills such as pronunciation and word recognition skills. I focus on phonetic analysis in order to assist the children in learning letter sounds."

"Mr. Marshall, what do you see yourself doing in the next ten years?" another female interviewer asked.

"I would like to be an Educational Psychologist. I believe that I can help our children even more, particularly the underachievers," I replied beaming with awe.

The other members of the panel inquired about whether I had applied for study leave, when I completed my studies and which age group I was teaching at the time.

"How long have you been teaching?" the chairperson asked.

"It is thirteen years that I have been teaching," I responded bravely.

"In what year did you complete the Erdiston Teachers' Training course?"

"My training was completed in 1991," I replied.

The interview was interspersed with inaudible exchanges among the panel members. Some of them flipped through the documents that were in front of them.

The chairperson quickly thanked me for attending and then said, "You will be hearing from us."

"Thank you very much," I replied.

The secretary approached me and beckoned the way out. I gathered my belongings and followed her.

What a relief! I thought.

After not hearing anything more, I dismissed the thought of being awarded a scholarship. It was early November. The Ministry of Education, in conjunction with the University of

West Indies, had requested the specialist Mathematics teachers in the primary schools to attend a seminar-type workshop. On that occasion, we were asked to prepare test items in Mathematics to be used in a pilot project for a government initiative called (Educational Technology) EDUTECH. The day was long, arduous, and draining. We wrote numerous Mathematics questions and sums. We reviewed them. The chairperson rechecked them. Then we rewrote the unaccepted ones. It was too much for one day.

On arriving home, my wife, Maria, told me in a rather casual manner, "A lady from the scholarship department called to say that you have been awarded a scholarship. She asked you to give her a call on Monday."

"What! I got the scholarship?" I asked quietly.

"That's what you wanted," Maria replied, as she stared at me.

"I did. But I had put it out of my mind after I didn't hear anything more," I answered, chipping in with a low tone of voice.

The good news had arrived. It was unbelievable. I anxiously craved for the weekend to come and go so that I could hear the news for myself. The news was not absorbed as yet. I spent my weekend in apprehension. *Is it really true? Did I really get the scholarship? I have to hear this for myself.* A million and one thoughts permeated my mind.

It was Monday morning. I prepared as usual for school, took my wife to work and dropped my son off on the way. Having arrived at school, I assembled the children for morning worship and ensured that they were supervised throughout the fifteen minute session. Immediately after the worship, I asked my colleague who had students of a similar age-group to mine, to supervise them for me as they returned to the classroom. I briskly walked to the office. I dialled the telephone number for the Ministry of Education and asked the receptionist to allow me to speak with the officer who had called for me on the previous Friday. In a few minutes, a calm voice on the other end of the line queried, "Mr. Marshall?"

"Sure, I am returning your call from Friday," I replied.

"I called to let you know that you have been awarded a National Development Scholarship and you are expected to travel in January," she said.

"Oh, thank you very much," I responded.

"You will need to come in so that I can discuss the conditions with you as soon as possible," she answered.

"Ok. Let me get back to you some time this week," I responded.

I put back the receiver, rushed over to the quadrangle (the area of the school where assembly was held) only to find a few teachers, along with the principal, chatting. With tears streaming from my eyes, I said, "I won a National Development Scholarship."

Penelope screamed and rushed to me with outstretched arms, "Marsh, you got it. Congratulations!"

The tears would not stop. Cindy, smiling broadly, stormed through with a hug and exclaimed, "I knew you would get it!"

By this time the principal had outstretched her hand to congratulate me with a hand shake, "Well done."

Sheila, who was waiting her turn, burst into the group to give me a huge hug. "Congrats! You worked hard to get there."

Time was slipping away. My students were with my other colleague and I had to fetch them to relieve her. On arriving at her classroom, I found her busy engaging the entire group of students in spelling and Arithmetic drills. She saw my tearful eyes. And so did a few very observant 7-8 year old students.

"Sir is crying," said Chade, the boldest of the students.

"What's wrong?" my colleague asked, now getting a chance.

"I was awarded a National Development Scholarship." I responded, wiping my tears away.

"Ahhhhhhhhhhhh!" she screamed and hugged me instantly.

On recognising that we still had to teach, she told me that she would talk with me later. I collected my students and proceeded to my classroom. I managed to compose myself. The thought of the scholarship was still fresh in my mind. But I kept focused and got on with my teaching assignments for the day. I was awarded a scholarship so that I could pursue my Master's. I was elated. My heart was bubbling. I was truly thankful for this divine move on my behalf, when I least expected it. But it was the beginning of an unforgettable journey!

September 1999 was a turning point in my life: ever since then, things have been happening. It was during this time that I prepared to embark on my studies overseas. I arranged my flight and sorted out my finances with the scholarship department. I departed for the United Kingdom to pursue a Master's of Education in Special Need Education. From all appearances, I had planned to return to the Caribbean by September 2000 to resume my teaching duties, share the knowledge gained and utilise the skills acquired. More importantly, my wife, Maria and son, Josiah were expecting me back within a year, but this was not to be, at least not for the short term.

By December 1999, the Lord was speaking to me about various issues. One particular text that helped me put some of the issues into perspective is St. Matthew 26:39 which reads "He went a little farther and fell on His face, and prayed, saying, 'O My Father, if it be possible, let this cup pass from

Me; nevertheless, not as I will, but as You will'" (NKJV). In this prayer of agony, Jesus was honest about His willingness to die on the cross. I felt the Lord was also asking me to be honest about His apparent plan for my life. As time rushed by, a relationship between a number of newfound friends and myself began to develop. In the group were two sets of sisters: one set, Jean and Idamay from the African continent and Jenny and Julie from the Caribbean. There were four from the Uk: Judy, Pat, Lynette and Noveline. And there was also Roy who was also from the Caribbean. All of us, except for Pat, were studying. We were a zealous army of young people who were eager to participate in outreach activities. We were eager to develop our spirituality through bible studies and prayer sessions. We longed to assist other young people, like ourselves, in believing and accepting Jesus. Instinctively, I reached out to many of them. I found myself actively encouraging some of the youth to get involve in early morning worship. It was this initiative that paved the way for me to come face to face with God's mission for me. In deed, our God-given gifts are essential to the spiritual progress and development of others with whom we associate. We have to agree that the gifts were distributed "for the equipping of the saints for the work of ministry, for the edifying of the body of Christ, till we all come to the unity of the faith and of the knowledge of the Son of God, to a perfect man, to the measure of the stature of the fullness of Christ; that we should no longer be children, tossed to and fro and carried about with every wind of doctrine, by the trickery of men, in the cunning craftiness of deceitful plotting, but, speaking the truth in love, may grow up in all things into Him who is the head—Christ—from whom the whole body, joined and knit together by what every joint supplies, according to the effective working by which every part does its share, causes growth of the body for the edifying of itself in love" (Eph 4;12-16, NKJV). Those who hold this perspective are eager to become involve in whatever activity is necessary to ensure that lives are changed.

Other texts that I was inspired to read and study (Jeremiah 3; Daniel 6) hinted that the Lord had something in store of which I was still spiritually unaware. As I studied St. Matthew 14:22-34, which reads, "Immediately Jesus made His disciples get into the boat and go before Him to the other side, while He sent the multitudes away. And when He had sent the multitudes away, He went up on the mountain by Himself to pray. Now when evening came, He was alone there. But the boat was now in the middle of the sea, tossed by the waves, for the wind was contrary. Now in the fourth watch of the night Jesus went to them, walking on the sea. And when the disciples saw Him walking on the sea, they were troubled, saying, 'It is a ghost!' And they cried out for fear. But immediately Jesus spoke to them, saying, 'Be of good cheer! It is I; do not be afraid.' And Peter answered Him and said, 'Lord, if it is You, command me to come to You on the water.' So He said, 'Come.' And when Peter had come down out of the boat, he walked on the water to go to Jesus. But when he saw that the wind *was* boisterous, he was afraid; and beginning to sink he cried out, saying, 'Lord, save me!' And immediately Jesus stretched out [*His*] hand and caught him, and said to him, 'O you of little faith, why did you doubt?' And when they got into the boat, the wind ceased. Then those who were in the boat came and worshiped Him, saying, 'Truly You are the Son of God.' When they had crossed over, they came to the land of Gennesaret" (NKJV), the Lord seemed to have been speaking to me explicitly about the dangers and difficulties that I would encounter on His mission. I noted the following in my prayer journal: *I cannot step out if the Lord does not prepare me. He rebuked Peter for a lack of faith, but on the contrary, I asked that He would provide me with a stronger faith. I continued to take in the message. Did Peter know for what he was asking? When the Lord says go, we should go.*

But, then, when I examined the text closer, I realised that, had the winds started before the disciples went out to sea, they may never have pushed off. At times, the Lord hides events from us and only asks that we move by faith. I notice that Jesus walked through the troubled sea because He is the Master of the sea. As He walked, Peter, on recognising that it was Him, wanted to go to Jesus. His ego seemed to have surfaced and his extroverted personality instigated the impulsive request, "Lord, if it's you, tell me to come to you on the water" (Mt 14:28, NIV). So, Jesus said, "Come!" (verse 29). (Be careful what you ask for!) Our emotional instability can be a hindrance to our spiritual progress and maturity. We don't see the negative impact. We don't monitor ourselves emotionally. In the end, it is because of this emotional condition that we come up short of our true potential.

Just as Peter had accomplished a great feat, which only Jesus had done, we, too, can accomplish the impossible for Jesus. We should not be afraid, because He did not equip us with "a spirit of fear, but of power, and of love and of a sound mind" (2 Tim 1:7). In comparing Peter's experience to mine, I realise that I had to be prepared for boisterous winds and disappointments that would come my way. It does not matter how well prepared we are, in moments of difficulties, we are never emotionally or psychologically equipped. Our human frailty surfaces and we tend to exhibit behaviours similar to the ungodly. Without the grace of God, we will sink in the pool of trials. We splash like a drowning person because our experiences are in contrast to our perspective in life. It's our circumstances in life that tend to dictate our perspective. In this text, the Holy Spirit also revealed that, sometimes, the Lord sends us through rough patches, but He watches over us and gives us the necessary grace, even though He does not always makes the path smooth.

While Jesus is working in, on, and through us, the adversary is also at work. But Jesus is always watching over us, even when trouble comes. I asked myself, "Why did Peter want to leave the others?" I believed he wanted a special experience. Do you feel like pulling out from the familiar surroundings for a while to be with Jesus so that you too can gain a new experience? Until you have the desire you will never ask for something more or move beyond your present position. Finally, from the text, the Holy Spirit comforted me with the thought that I should not doubt because since the Lord called me, like Peter, He will provide for me. The Holy Ghost also revealed to me that Jesus will make a way for me and that he will open opportunities when it seems as though I am going under.

It is interesting to note that this bold and impulsive disciple cried out, "Lord save me"(Mt 14:30). Where did all his pomp and robustness go in the face of stark calamities? When failures come our way and we feel as though we are sinking, we too, should plead with Jesus, the One who created us, who owns the whole world and gave his life for us. Our world may seem to be falling apart, or we may feel suicidal, but I want to assure you that we can find the comfort we long for in allowing the God of Heaven to have a chance in our lives. The words of the song penned by Maltbie Babcock (1901) rushes to my mind: "This is my Father's world; why should my hear be sad? The Lord is King" and brings hope to my heart.

These devotional texts are filled with stirring insights and messages that the Lord was using to prepare me for His task. I was engulfed in intense prayer, consistent morning devotions, and the study of God's word. Although I was in my upper room, I had not yet felt the real desire to seek the Lord about His purpose for me. The inspiration to engage in personal devotions was timely and critical to all that would follow because it paved the way for my new role with some of the other young people. Personal devotions are of paramount importance since we are supplied with an adequate portion of fresh spiritual food, which can be shared with others.[4] We become rejuvenated for the day ahead and we are better prepared to face the challenges, the trials, and the apparent disappointments that we may face in a day. Moreover, Ellen White advises that "all who are under the training of God need the quiet hour for communion with their own hearts, with nature and with God."[5] I am thankful for the desire that was put in my heart to have 'family worship' with some of these young people because it helped us renew our connections with the source of our Christian love, and that is Christ.

After Jesus' ascension, Luke, the author of the Third Gospel tells us that the disciples "went up into an upper room, where abode both Peter, and James, and John, and Andrew, Philip, and Thomas, Bartholomew, and Matthew, James *the son* of Alphaeus, and Simon Zelotes, and Judas *the brother* of James. These all continued with one accord in prayer and supplication, with the women, and Mary the mother of Jesus, and with his brethren" (Acts 1:13-14, NJKV). It was only then that the disciples came to grips with Jesus' earlier invitation. They re-grouped in their upper room and remained there with one goal. They engaged in many prayer sessions and also engaged in other personal preparation. According to John T. Squires, "this was a community that met continuously during these ten days. The constant and communal nature of their meetings will later become important. Such continuity is an implicit element in God's ongoing sovereignty."[6] It is evident from their actions and attitude that they were willing to wait on the Lord. They wanted a spiritual change. Moreover, their activities in the upper room suggested that they were desperate and longing for Jesus to meet their spiritual needs. They put aside the biases, the desire to be first, and killed their human egos so that the ministry and the apostle-ship (Acts 1:25) that were entrusted to them could be perceived positively. It was the beginning moment for them.

Human beings, even though they are of different personality traits, tend to resist divine intervention in their lives. Carver and Scheier conclude that it is the introverted individual who is rigid and unchanging in his behaviour and ideas.[7] Such individuals seldom see the 'bigger picture' because they are motivated by events in their inner world. What is your inner desire? Are you desperate for a new experience so that you may see God's tremendous power? Do you know what is God's purpose for your life? What attitude are you displaying at the moment? Is there a need for something more in your life? Is your life at a standstill? If you have a burning quest to know, plunge deeper into these inspired chapters and read on.

Taking Time For Reflection {Jot down your thoughts}

- What event(s) started you thinking about the direction in which your life was taking?

- In what direction is your life going?

- How far are you from achieving your personal dream or desire of your life?

- To what extent are you satisfied with where you are at the moment or with what you are doing?

- What steps do you plan to take to rectify or improve your situation?

- To what extent has this chapter helped you in your personal life?

2
Wrestling on My Knees

"Prayer is heaven's ordained means of success in the conflict with sin and the development of Christian character" (White, 1911: *Acts of the Apostles:* 564)

The confrontation between Jesus and Peter prompted the ultimate response, "Lord, you know all things; you know that I love you" (Jn 21:17, NIV). These sentiments echoed Peter's true feelings after the denial experience and the encounter on the sea-shores of Tiberias. These words seem to represent the pain and grief he felt in having to let go of his fishing trade. This was his passion, his dream, and his identity. He had been cut off from a life-long friend. He, along with the other disciples, found their upper room and spent quality time with their Lord, confessing their sins and searching the Scriptures [Old Testament]. Such an event illustrates the need to be alone with our Maker so we can reflect, hear His voice, and be refreshed. Through prayer, they attempted to bring their lives in harmony with God's word by earnestly requesting the power of the Holy Spirit.

The results? Fifty days after Jesus' ascension to his heavenly home, the praying disciples were blessed with God's anointing and with the gift of many languages. Luke recounts this dramatic event by reminding us that "Suddenly a sound like the blowing of a violent wind came from heaven and filled the whole house where they were sitting. They saw what seemed to be tongues of fire that separated and came to rest on each of them. All of them were filled with the Holy Spirit and began to speak in other tongues as the Spirit enabled them" (Acts 2:2-4, NKJV). This prayer phase provided a spiritual experience that transformed their lives and by extension, the lives of those who believed on Jesus through their words. That day was the high point in the disciples' lives. It illustrated to them and to those around that there was someone who still specialised in miraculously transforming lives. It was undoubtedly a manifestation of divine power. They were on course, fulfilling the mission of Acts1:8, where Luke reminds us that Jesus told the disciples that they "shall receive power when the Holy Spirit has come upon you; and you shall be witnesses to

Me in Jerusalem, and in all Judea and Samaria, and to the end of the earth" (NKJV). They were determined to see it to completion.

The religious, political, and social world since then was never the same, seeing that people of all walks of life had experienced a change in their life-styles. A new day had dawned for many citizens of various nations during the times of the Apostles. These nationals saw the apostles functioning in capacities and with capabilities that were beyond their social and educational background. The writer of Acts pointedly reminds us that some of the people on the Day of Pentecost "came together in bewilderment, because each one heard them speaking in his own language. Utterly amazed, they asked, 'Are not all these men who are speaking Galileans? Then how is it that each of us hears them in his own native language?'" (Acts 2:6-8,NIV. John T. Squires asserts that "the foreign languages which were spoken begin to fulfil Jesus' prediction that the message was to be preached in every nation."[8] Responding to divine guidance brings about expanded territory which we least expected. It's in this territory that our purpose becomes fulfilled and we feel at peace within, knowing that a difference is being accomplished.

It was in January 2000 when the Lord confronted me concerning a number of issues. As I engaged in regular morning devotions, the theme of righteousness was the focus of many of the messages. My prayer life continued to blossom as I was strengthened with instructions and messages from 2 Tim. 3, Mt. 12, and other biblical texts. The kind of prayer that I was engaged in exposed my past, brought my forgotten sinful behaviour to the surface, and led me on to a path of deep and painful repentance. Was it that I hadn't repented before? It wasn't that. I saw who I really was, the enormity of my cruel, selfish, and indulging behaviour. I saw how I hurt others, along with Jesus, my Redeemer. Tears from my fatigued eyes streamed down my sombre cheeks as I faced my past constantly. They trickled down my cheeks like a busted dam. I was broken and helpless, but the compassionate Saviour comforted, forgave, and lifted me up to begin a new journey.

The Lord reminded me often to keep the faith. The intensity of God's preparation for something big for me was evident also from Daniel 6 and Luke 8. Through these chapters, the Lord revealed to me that He was going to protect me as long as I did His bidding. I did not fully understand what was happening. I took these sessions as being normal, seeing that I desired to draw nearer to the Lord in my Christian walk. Does God always open back the curtains of the future for us to peer in to the distant? It is evident from my experiences that He urges us to trust Him, to be faithful so that He may lead us step by step. Our human desire to be in control suggests that we need to know what's ahead. It's about having the need for power. Power to control our destiny, our lives, and how our plans are shaped and in what ways they succeed. Here is precisely the reason why the curtains of the future are kept close because "in his heart a man plans his course, but the Lord determines his steps (Prov. 16:9, NIV).

From studying the various devotional texts, I gleaned that many individuals will scoff at and oppose my decision, but, like Daniel, God wanted me to obey. It is such experiences that expose our personality traits. Can we handle the ridicule? How will we move beyond the harsh words of others? Our inner strength, mental capacity and patience come under severe scrutiny. Our resilience in times of personal difficulty is carried through the grinding mill. We come to perceive the benefit of spending time in prayer and meditation. It's indispensable to the heart that is searching for more. It is only through the power of prevailing prayer that we become spiritually victorious. We gain inner spiritual strength. We feel powerful. Our thoughts move from the negative to the positive zone. But, apart from an intense prayer life, we must arise from prayer and act in faith.

Further insights from God's word indicate to me that one should always look out for the answer to prayers even when all situations appear to be hopeless. Here is where our faith must rise to the challenge, holding firmly to his promises while our eyes are on him. The record in 2 Chronicles reminds us of Jehosophat's experience and his seemingly hopeless situation. Men of prayer have an inner conviction that would not allow them to surrender or to succumb to life's difficulties. Richard J. Coggins views Jehosophat's response to the invasion as a challenge and concludes that "in the face of this threat Jehosophat responds in a wholly admirable way, seeking the Lord, proclaiming a fast, and summoning the assembly to meet in the temple."[9] Amidst the nerve-racking obstacles, this

Judean King, trembling in his boots, resolved to inquire of the Lord. The writer of the narrative, in depicting the drama, recalls that "Jehoshaphat feared, and set himself to seek the LORD, and proclaimed a fast throughout all Judah" (2 Chron.20:3,NKJV). Having addressed the nation, he declared a day of prayer and mourning and led the prayer session with a 221-word intercessory prayer "O LORD God of our fathers, *are* [sic] You not God in heaven, and do You *not* [sic] rule over all the kingdoms of the nations, and in Your hand *is there not*[sic] power and might, so that no one is able to withstand You? *Are* You not our God, who drove out the inhabitants of this land before Your people Israel, and gave it to the descendants of Abraham Your friend forever? And they dwell in it, and have built You a sanctuary in it for Your name, saying, 'If disaster comes upon us—sword, judgment, pestilence, or famine—we will stand before this temple and in Your presence (for Your name *is* in this temple), and cry out to You in our affliction, and You will hear and save.'" (verses 6-9, NKJ. This bold regal Judean leader was adamant. The degree of assertion propelled him to say, "And now, here are the people of Ammon, Moab, and Mount Seir—whom You would not let Israel invade when they came out of the land of Egypt, but they turned from them and did not destroy them; here they are, rewarding us by coming to throw us out of Your possession which You have given us to inherit. O our God, will You not judge them? For we have no power against this great multitude that is coming against us; nor do we know what to do, but our eyes *are* upon You." (verses 10-12, NKJV). His heart throbbed while the armies of the enemy marched forward as a trio, but he admitted his weakness and insufficiency, "For we have no power to face this vast army that is attacking us. We do not know what to do, but our eyes are upon you" (2 Chron. 20:12,NIV). Such is the resolve of mighty prayer warriors who step out into the unknown in spite of the absence of solutions to the human mind.

There were times when my prayers turned to praise, through faith in Yahweh, knowing that He had heard and would answer my prayer. During these moments, biblical texts such as "Delight thyself also in the LORD; and he shall give thee the desires of thine heart" (Ps. 37:4) and "Cast thy burden upon the LORD, and he shall sustain thee: he shall never suffer the righteous to be moved" (Ps. 55:22) were like water to a thirsty soul on a hot day. I was comforted while the harsh reality of life pressed down on me. But it wasn't always pain. There were many moments of joy and laughter. Knowing that there are friends to empathise with us and walk with us in prayer is therapeutically advantageous. Being in the presence of people with similar visions and similar experiences boost our moral, awakens the spiritual ego within our hearts, and motivates us to move ahead.

Ezekiel 10: 9-10 portrays Jesus as being the central force of all things which are happening around me. Based on this biblical perspective, I became aware that my life revolves around God, His missionary work and His will for my life. He is "like a wheel intersecting a wheel" (verse 10). It is He who turns our lives in whatever direction He determines. It's solemn to realise that we are like clay moulded into selected vessels by the potter. Although the question is posed: "Does the clay say to the potter, What are you making?" (Isa. 45:9, NIV), the prophet Isaiah declares, "Yet, O Lord, you are our Father. We are the clay, you are the potter; we are all the work of your hand" (64.8,NIV). From these texts, I perceive the Lord was saying that His hands are the guiding instrument in my life. As long as I am attached to Him, the victory would be mine.

Within three months, I felt the need to seek the Lord in prayer and fasting again. Why? The Lord had impressed on my mind that there was a spiritual need among the youth at my new home-church in the United Kingdom. Judges 6 was the first text that helped me to put this new leading into perspective. It is here that the writes commences the encounter between God and Gideon. The author of Judges informs us that "the Angel of the LORD came and sat under the terebinth tree which *was* in Ophrah, which *belonged* [sic] to Joash the Abiezrite, while his son Gideon threshed wheat in the winepress, in order to hide *it* from the Midianites. And the Angel of the LORD appeared to him, and said to him, 'The LORD *is* with you, you mighty man of valor!' Gideon said to Him, 'O my lord, if the LORD is with us, why then has all this happened to us? And where *are*[sic] all His miracles which our fathers told us about, saying, 'Did not the LORD bring us up from Egypt?' But now the LORD has forsaken us and delivered us into the hands of the Midianites.' Then the LORD turned to him and said, 'Go in this might of yours, and you shall save Israel from the hand of the Midianites. Have I not sent you?'" (Judges 6:11-14,NKJV). I realised that Gideon wanted to be certain of the Lord's plan to use him to save the Israelites from the hands of the mighty and vicious warring neighbours. What was the real purpose of the text for me? Rationalisation and logic are two philosophical tools we use when we least expect God to come into our lives. It was similar with Gideon who, in wanting to be certain of his divine call, demanded, "If now I have found favor in Your sight, then show me a sign that it is You who talk with me" (6:17, NKJV).

I approached the Lord with a fourteen-item list of which two were answered within a day, one within two and-a half months and nine months later another one. Most of these were for my church friends. There were many tough decisions to be made. I had to take time to intercede about each decision. Lives were at stake and one wrong move could cause an entire army of young people to miss out on something special. Many days were spent reflecting, meditating, and thinking through these decisions. They required careful thought and with time, according to God's will, there were results.

One day per week was spent in fasting. It was during this time that I was confronted with the decision of whether I should return to my Caribbean home country after my year of studies or 'work' with the young people. This was a major decision in that it involved my family, my job and all of my financial commitments back in my Caribbean home. When we are caught between our world and the world that God wants to lead us into, we are caught on our cross-roads. Often times we are not sure of the direction to take. The heart and head tug for supremacy. How do we know which direction to take? The more serious the decision, the more frequent and the longer we should pray and fast. There were many other personal and miscellaneous issues that I had to grapple with, thus reinforcing the need for me to remain in prayer and fasting.

Why do I want to stay in the UK? I asked myself.

Clearly, the Lord had shown me that the youth needed help, so I went to him in prayer about it. As I reached out to the Lord, issues such as the resumption of my teaching duties with the Ministry of Education and my family always stared me in the face. Was I trapped beyond escape?

Lord, what is your plan for me? Is it your will for me to stay in the United Kingdom were the questions I raised.

I wasn't sure. I knew that there was a need for someone spiritually strong to encourage, guide, motivate, and help evangelise the youth. In sum, there was a need for someone to conduct in-reach evangelism. Youngberg & Youngberg described this kind of activity as standing in the gap so that God's children can "reclaim the ground that others have yielded to the enemy...and to join Him in His great quest of saving others."[10]

My role was opposite to the Lord's declaration over the Israelites when He spoke through the prophet Ezekiel, saying, "...and I sought for a man among them, that should...stand in the gap before me for that land...but I found none" (ch 22:3). There was need for someone to intercede for and provide prayerful support for God's people. Wrestling on our knees for each other is the greatest spiritual activity in which we participate. The prayer phase puts focus on our activities. We sense a move in the right direction. It's in this way that our purpose in life begins to evolve and we begin to see where we fit in, while becoming prepared for that awesome responsibility.

Intercessory work is of paramount importance to the lives of God's creatures. Isaiah contended that God wanted someone to stand up for his people, but "he saw that there was no one, he was appalled that there was no one to intervene; so his own arm worked salvation for him, and his own righteousness sustained him" (59:16, NIV). In humility, I must admit that I had five years of solid experience in mentoring, which came about through my working with the different groups of new converts prior to my arrival in the UK. In retrospect, this experience prepared me for this new mission with the youth, with whom I was closely connected. Was I the only person with the needed skills? This was certainly not the case.

It seemed at the time that no one was willing to 'stand in the gap' for God's people. I was willing, if not able. But how was I supposed to know exactly that this was God's will? What solutions did I have for this dilemma? Some of the things I wrote in my journal are: *Pray that God will give someone else the same vision (but I would be excusing myself from a task which the Lord has presented to me). Teach the youth, encourage them and trust that they would obtain the skills (tactfulness, discernment) and attitude (caring, sensitivity). But we all have different gifts and therefore, even if I guided them along this path, these gifts may still be missing. Go back home, get on with my life and work with the youth at home. But the vision is not for my home country. Forget about it. This would be disobedience. Go home and write back often. But how effective is this? Everyone is busy and we all may lapse into our old way of doing things and lose the motivation. Will they respond promptly to my letters? Wouldn't it be trying to force something on individuals, when I don't know what the situation is like? Is it not preferable to be on the spot? Has anyone else seen what you have seen? Are they willing to take on the task? Accept the challenge, stay and be committed to working with God's people.*

Within one month, I was convinced that the vision was for the UK and not for my home country. Moreover, the spiritual situation that prevailed at the time required someone, through much prayer, to encourage and assist the youth in being faithful and in being committed. This group of young people needed intercessory prayers. According to Youngberg & Youngberg (1994), "intercession brings supernatural allies to battle. The discouraged and the disheartened find new strength and those under bondage to the enemy are freed."[11] Freedom and revival came our way. I realised that "intercessory prayer makes a difference."[12]

By this time, we had formed a missionary group called ACTION 2000, a sub-group of the local Adventist Youth Society department. We engaged in activities such as prayer walking, door-to-door tract distribution and half-night prayer meetings. With the passage of time, I came to recognise that there was a principal and a secondary problem. By what means was I going to stay in the UK, seeing that I was bonded to the government from the award of a scholarship? Should I study or work? After careful consideration, I was impressed to study full time. I quickly set about preparing my application form for doctoral studies. Meanwhile, I knew that there were no personal funds for the studies (£20,000 for the 3 years), so I applied for as many scholarships as I could.

Other major concerns emerged: renewal of my student visa and what to do about my wife, Maria and son, Josiah, whom I had left in the Caribbean. These matters were being prayed about constantly: within two months, the Lord had opened two college doors for my wife to come and study, while paying a very small fee of three hundred pounds per year. I returned home on holiday. During that time, my wife and I discussed and prayed about the plan. She agreed to the plan and assured me that she would come as soon as things were in place (house and visa). I praise my Heavenly Father for my wife's willingness to give me up for this cause.

Since this decision meant total sacrifice and possible censure from the government, I assessed the time it would take for the mission to finish. How long will it take? How long do I want to stay in the UK? These were the questioned that flooded my mind. I answered rhetorically: "until the mission is finished." The goal was clear and so was the purpose. How much more intense could such a dilemma be, knowing that the Lord has placed a burden on my heart? Within two months of my prayer and fasting session, the university where I was studying recommended me to pursue PhD studies. Another university about thirty miles away also gave me a place on its PhD programme. I was elated and ecstatic and so too were my fellow young people. They showered congratulations on me from every corner. Meanwhile, I focused on my immediate studies, often times lifting the assignments to the Lord in prayer, through the application of the Hezekiah principle. During another prayer and fasting session, I brought a thirteen-item list to the Lord of which one was answered one week later. Pressure was building up as my M Ed programme was coming to a close. A 15000-word thesis had to be completed and so I had to pull out all the 'stops'.

Through Exodus 14, the Lord had comforted me by re-assuring me that He would fight my battles, if I would only stand still and see His salvation. In studying the following text, "Leaving the crowd behind, they took him along, just as he was, in the boat. There were also other boats with him. A furious squall came up, and the waves broke over the boat, so that it was nearly swamped. Jesus was in the stern, sleeping on a cushion. The disciples woke him and said to him, 'Teacher, don't you care if we drown?' He got up, rebuked the wind and said to the waves, 'Quiet! Be still!' Then the wind died down and it was completely calm. He said to his disciples, 'Why are you so afraid? Do you still have no faith?' They were terrified and asked each other, 'Who is this? Even the wind and the waves obey him!'" (Mk. 4:36-41, NIV), the Holy Spirit showed me that it is the Lord who opens the way and therefore, when difficulties come, call on Him, just as the desperate stormed-trapped disciples did on the boisterous sea. Indeed, He cares for us. If He could speak to the elements (wind and sea waves), how much more can He not speak to the minds and thoughts of individuals. My yearnings were explained in the text, "teach me to do thy will; for thou art my God: thy spirit is good; lead me into the land of uprightness" (Ps 143:10) since it was my desire to know God's will for my life.

I wrestled with the God of Heaven often and long, sometimes into the early hours of the morning because I needed answers. Like Jacob, I vehemently said that "I will not let you go unless you bless me" (Gen. 32:26, NIV). But do you think that brought any answers? No, it didn't. But it brought me closer to God, allowing me to hear His voice and feel His presence. It wasn't a case of rising up before dawn or staying late at night looking for a way out of my troubles because I was well aware that "he [God] grants sleep to those he loves" (Psalm 127:2, NIV).

During this mountainous ordeal, God had helped me to see that I should not be thinking *about* the situation, but I should be thinking *through* it. The difference is when we think *about* our problems, nothing changes except us. We become mentally imbalanced and disturbed, lose weight, and our hair turns grey. On the other hand, thinking *through* means to look at different ways to solve the situation. We examine it from many angles. However, most times after we have searched hard and long, we still don't find the solution. That's when the Holy Spirit shows up and reveals a way out that we never had in our minds.

Through prayer and a willing spirit, I was certain about God's plan for my life. As we spend time in prayer, the Holy Spirit enlightens us and makes some of our situations clearer. We become more focused, more purposeful, and more determined to allow God's will to be accomplished in our lives. So where are you in the scheme of things? What psychological battles are you fighting? Are you convinced of what is your purpose in life? I want to challenge you to spend some time in reflection, admit that you are discontented with your position and with what you have. Ask: 'Lord, what will thou have me to do?' Prayer is the key!

<u>Taking Time For Reflection</u> {Jot down your thoughts}

- What is it in your life that you demand urgent help with?

- Having read these two chapters so far, what avenues or steps can you take that would aid you with what you said concerning the question above?

- How important is it for you to ask someone to help you explore these avenues? Why do you say that?

- What is it in this chapter that has inspired you deeply?

- You have no doubt read and probably re-read this chapter. What is your resolve at this moment about what you have read?

- What challenges have you come across after reading this chapter?

3

"Signs! Signs! and more Signs!"

"If trials increase upon them...God is testing and proving their fidelity"

(The Youth's Instructor, March 1878, quoted in White, *Messages to Young People*, 1958:80)

How do we know that the Lord have a specific task for us? How does He signal His purpose for our lives? At times, we struggle to achieve big things in this life. But the God of Heaven knows our hearts and He controls the future. He signals to us through a variety of ways what is His purpose for us. He has a particular purpose for our lives. If we long to obey Him sincerely, He will not let us rest, neither will He allow us to veer off-course forever. For example, Gideon, in the book of Judges, yearned for a sign because he wanted to be sure that the Lord was calling him. We too can ask for a sign! Nevertheless, there are signs in our lives that point us in a particular direction. But we ignore the flashes.

Simon Peter, the PRO (Public Relations Officer/spokesman) for the disciples decided that he was reverting to his old profession. He boldly declared, "I go a fishing" (Jn 21:3). What propelled him to return to the calm lake? Did he succeed? Did his efforts that night gain him any blessings or happiness? From this text, it is clear that he, along with the other disciples who went along with him were disappointed. What was the reason?

Their nets and fishing rods came up empty. It is in times like these that we come to the realisation that Jesus is right when He says, "I am the vine, ye are the branches: He that abideth in me, and I in him, the same bringeth forth much fruit: for without me ye can do nothing" (Jn 15:5). Kenneth Maahs, in commenting, notes that "Such a trip to familiar settings and relaxing endeavors would surely be in keeping with both their physical, psychological, and emotional needs."[13] Peter's personality would not allow him to glare at the high seas and not venture out. The adventurous trip cost him. Ultimately, he gained nothing for his hard nocturnal labour.

But that's what the Lord does to attract our attention and to re-direct our flight so that we can be focused on the mission. Since Peter was the spokesman, the other six disciples, without giving much thought to the suggestion, fell for it and followed blindly. From Bruce Milne's perspective, "In terms of their psychological and emotional well-being, a fishing expedition back in the old familiar surroundings of the Sea of Galilee was therapeutically ideal."[14] Maybe they jelled together as a group once more by participating wholeheartedly in a familiar business enterprise for which they had a burning passion. In the end, they too suffered the great loss. Can we afford to listen to individuals who didn't hear the voice of Jesus? Should we submit to our friends who, though sincere with their advice as much as possible, are uncertain about God's purpose for our lives? It is an individual experience.

Could the disciples have been in the ship all night and be satisfied with nothing? Certainly not! I believe Jesus must have up-braided Peter with extra words such as: 'Peter, although your heart is on the fish, that's not what I call you to do.' In spite of the stark failures that stare us in the eye, we struggle in an attempt to grasp at the last straw, hoping to succeed.

There is a valuable lesson here: When God calls, we should respond obediently. At times, we have to learn the hard way: excruciating pain, profound grief, devastating disappointments and a slide down a precipice in order to bring us back to our senses. In his mercies, he still gives us grace to go through our fires and floods. He soothes the galling wounds, but we must bear the pain and grief, which are the consequences of our actions.

The confrontation between Jesus and the seven disciples on the seashores of Tiberias was an opportune moment for the disciples to reconsider Jesus' earlier invitation: "I am going to send you what my Father has promised: but stay in the city until you have been clothed with power from on high" (Lk.24:49, NIV). It was these unexpected and harsh disappointments that forced the distraught disciples to come to grips with Jesus' purpose for their lives. As Jesus outlined His plan to Peter specifically, the impulsiveness vanished and he surrendered without a fight: "Lord, though knowest that I love thee" (Jn 21: 17). How was the Lord going to reveal to me that it was His will for me to stay in the UK? I didn't have a clue. As time for registration approached and with me still seeking funding, I decided to engage in prayer and fasting in September 2000. My prayer list was twelve items long. It was one of the most devastating prayer and fasting sessions I have had up to this time. The time was spent weeping before the God of Heaven. There was immense pressure. I was stressed out. I agonised over the many issues. I cried and groaned. I was broken, weak, and helpless. No one could help but Jesus.

When I arrived in the UK in September 1999, a well-built immigration officer granted me a one-year student visa. Now, the time to renew my visa had arrived. Since I did not have six thousand pounds to pay for the first year of my doctoral studies,

I decided to pray for full funding and a three-year visa among many other things. By October, Paula, a close friend of mine, had lent me £2000. It was calm autumn afternoon when Paula and I were chatting about our plans that the subject of my studies popped up. She had come to my office at the university to visit me. The layout in the office was simple. There were five large study tables and three book shelves along with a microwave oven and an electrical kettle. It was overlooking one of the car parks. Some large trees provided a lively view. While sitting at one of the three almost obsolete computers that were assigned to the other five doctoral students and my self by my department, She posed a question.

"Were you able to get any funding as yet?" she enquired.

"No, I haven't," I replied reluctantly.

"So what are you going to do about registration?" she pushed.

"Well I am more worried about my visa, seeing that it is expired," I informed her.

"I have some money that I don't need now. I will lend you. Pay me whenever you get it."

"Are you sure?" I queried with a smile.

"Don't worry about it. I can lend you," she confirmed in a persistent manner.

"Thank you ever so much. I don't know what to say," I replied in a reserved manner.

We talked about my studies, but I never approached my friend about the money. It was done from choice. Was this divinely orchestrated or was this a means of giving help to the have-nots? I went on my knees and thanked Jehovah—Jireh, who is my provider. By this time, I was also given guaranteed work. I had been working tirelessly as a substitute teacher in various schools since April 2000. The teaching agency which employed me had given me a guarantee that they would provide teaching assignments at different schools for me daily or they would pay me eighty-five percent of the weekly wages. Praise the Lord for His mercies! The perception that the God of the Apostles is actively involved in our affairs allows us to attribute our achievements and disappointments to Him. But when He is passive in our lives, it becomes hard for us to see beyond the now. We look for answers in unexpected placed and within ourselves. What is even more devastating is when we perceive that mortals like ourselves are more apt to provide the solutions than the infinite Creator of the universe, who is God. It is a road we can very well avoid as it leads to philosophising divine sovereignty.

Although I was convinced that I should stay, the next few months were emotionally difficult for me. My wife, Maria, was not sure that she would join me. I missed them immensely, the Ministry of Education unequivocally had turned down my application for study leave and was threatening to fire me, and there were financial pressures. What was I to do? Graduation was nearby, but the weeks leading up to it were lived with bitter tears. Many nights I cried profusely. In the day time was no different. A week did not pass without me making a telephone call home. The many letters that I wrote did not fill the emptiness that was present. My heart was burdened by this time. I felt sad and disappointed that Maria and Josiah could not be at my side for the graduation. I had never in all my life missed my family like then. It was as though a part of my inner being had being torn from me.

On that fateful rainy, bleak December afternoon, I saw many students being accompanied by elderly individuals. There was no doubt that these were the students' parents. Others were walking with partners. It was suppose to be the climax of my long and hard year of studies. It was suppose to be a time of joy and elation. But a sense of dissatisfaction surrounded me. As we prepared to form a queue, it began to rain lightly. There were many students wearing different coloured graduation gowns. Soon after we had formed the queue, the ushers led us into the hall where the ceremony was held. We ambled up the aisle slowly, but together. I glanced up. The Vice Chancellor of the university, the Deans of our departments and the programme leaders were all wearing different coloured gowns as they stood motionlessly in their places on the platform. A special table was located in the centre of the platform. Our diplomas and certificates were delicately arranged on this table. Meanwhile, the guests were directed onto the upper section of the hall. Others were seated directly behind the BA students. As our names were called, I realised that we were seated in a special order. The recipients of doctoral degrees were at the front, followed by MPhil students, MA students, MEd and then those who were receiving undergraduate degrees. There was a sense of loneliness within me. But a decision on whether I would return home had to be made once and for all. Within my heart and with encouragement from my friends, I decided that the outcome of the visa application would determine my next move.

Moreover, I felt the need to go home to see my family. After discussions with my adopted family and my two loving and supportive pastors, I inquired about the earliest flight at a local travel agent. The attendant informed me that January 2, 2001 was the earliest. I wanted something sooner. There were no guarantees and a stand-by would have cost me. I settled for it. Up to this time, my visa had not yet been granted and the Christmas recess for most, if not all businesses was approaching. I was to travel in two weeks time. I sought help from the International Office of my university. The attendant relayed the news that the passport was found at the Immigration Department and that it was completed. Within me, I confidently uttered, "*Yes, Lord*," and punched my side with my elbow. Friday, the 22nd of December would be the last day for business.

When I reflect, it appears that my decision to return home was similar to Moses' return to his countrymen after he had spent valuable time in the 'backside of the desert' caring for Jethro's sheep (Ex. 3.1) Although Moses had fled Egypt and probably had suppressed any thoughts of his kinsmen, the Lord was watching carefully and He heard the cries of the Israelites' anguish and saw their oppression. The time for me to return to my family had come. I felt this opportunity would give me a bird's eye-view of the situation, allow me to understand my plight and also instil in me the need to carry out God's plan for me. Going home would give me a new perspective on the many issues I faced. It would be refreshing. It would restore my psychological stability, and be emotionally advantageous.

I woke up Sabbath morning. The large envelop lay on the floor after it was forced through the letter-box. I ripped it open. *Thank you Lord!* It was a three-year visa. My friends went wild. I was bubbling on the inside. It reinforced the need to trust in God and rely on his promises. The experience epitomises God's willingness to respond to our prayer and demonstrates His infinite power. In the meantime, the nominating committee had met to select individuals to carry out various church activities. Surprisingly, the chairperson had asked me to serve as an assistant youth leader, assistant Personal Ministries leader and Children's Division co-ordinator. The Lord was willing to use me in an official capacity, and I accepted them humbly.

My journey home was one with mixed feelings. I cried. Will I ever see my friends whom I had grown to love? Would I come back? There was much uncertainty. Nevertheless, while at home, my family and I prayed about our situation. We often discussed my desire to return to the UK. The Ministry of Education had instructed me to resume duties or be fired. Reason prevailed and I returned to the classroom. I was uncomfortable being back in the classroom. Within my heart, I knew this was not where I should be. Meanwhile, I tried every avenue to obtain study leave, but to no avail. I wrote letters to Service Commission, the Training Division and the Ministry of Education. My request for study leave was denied continuously. I was confident at this time that the Lord wanted me back in the UK. On the inside, I was unsatisfied in that the mission had not been accomplished. I felt it deeply within me. I knew I had to come back to the UK.

I chatted with my wife to ascertain how she felt. There was the need to know what was in her mind. I was willing to obey her suggestions, seeing she is the other half of me.

I remembered asking her, "What do you think I should do?"

"Are you sure it's the Lord, or you want to go back to your friends?" she asked bluntly.

"Why did you say that?" I replied.

She gave the assurance that she would support me in whatever decision was made. I responded by saying that the decision and sacrifice were going to be tough. Little did I know that it was truly going to be tough.

I resigned from the Government Teaching Service immediately, but with ambivalence. I knew I had to return to the UK, but I also realised that my family needed me. My home felt empty while I was there. I recognised that I was just passing through on my way back to my 'mission'. By doing this, I was giving up a job for life and a very good salary of $3200 at the time. My mind was fully made up and I went through with the decision. My son, Josiah, needed me. I could see it as clear as glass. We have been very close because he has always been my shadow wherever I went. If I was going for petrol, to the supermarket or for liquid petroleum gas for the stove, he would jump in the car with me. He was reaching a critical time in his life. It was soon time to prepare for the national test that would decide which secondary school he attends. I responded to God's bidding, committed my family into my Protector's (Jehovah-Nissi, The Lord, my Banner) arms and prayed that he would keep them safely. I returned to the UK in mid-January of 2001. Within a few weeks of my return, another prayer was answered. Then by February, I was given a £300 grant. Small though it was, we (my family, friends and I) gave God thanks for it. My family and friends distinctly said that there was more where that came from. I agreed.

Subsequently, in my earnest quest for funding, I explored the internet for organisations that give scholarships and grants. I remembered stumbling on an advertisement for a research assistant. This job would have provided me with enough money in return. To my disbelief, when I scrolled to the bottom of the page, the deadline was two days ago. I almost sunk in my seat immediately. My heart had lost the will to go on. My zeal had been quenched like water being thrown on a blazing hot fire. A few weeks later, I located another advertisement for a research assistant in Linguistics. Since I possess a BA degree in Linguistics, I was qualified for the job. Immediately, I completed the application form online. By this time, it was midnight and I could hear the strong, cold wintry breeze blowing briskly outside my office at the university. After downloading the completed application form, I rushed to my flat, placed the form in an envelope and carefully inscribed the recipient's address on the front side of the envelope. Early the next morning, I scampered hurriedly to the post office so that the application could be despatched to its destination before 12 noon. What made the errand more urgent was that the following Monday would be the deadline and I needed to have my application in the post very early. I paid enough postage to ensure that my application arrive by noon of the following Monday.

I anxiously waited for the weekend. It did pass. And a few more days also passed. I checked my emails one morning. The contents of the email shocked me out of my bones. The head of the Linguistics department had emailed to say that she had scrutinised my application and liked it very much, but that it had arrived too late. I was dumbfounded. I was stunned. There was a need for an explanation. So I replied to her. I informed her that I had paid the postage that guaranteed the application to reach her by 12 noon on the Monday. In her reply, she acknowledged that it did reached the university on time, but that it had been addressed to the incorrect section of her department, hence the reason for her receiving it after the deadline. I could have blown the thick, tightly sealed roof with my screams. Unbelievable! Nothing could be done. Another opportunity had escaped my desperate grasp.

Subsequently, a string of 'No!', 'No!', 'No!' to all of efforts in securing funds entangled me. *What was the Lord saying to me? Why was I not obtaining the funds?* I longed to pursue the doctoral programme and I went after it with all my heart and with renewed zeal. My philosophy at the time was 'I will do everything honestly that is in my power and the Lord will do the rest'. By March, the Lord had responded favourably to another prayer request. In June of that same year, the house that I prayed for (£300 monthly rent, three bedrooms, and central heating) was available. I was moved by God's response to my prayer. He provided the exact thing that I wanted. But I was also cautious.

By this time I was bankrupt. Even though I was working every day, there was no money available. I went back to my Redeemer. "Lord, what are you saying to me? You have provided the house, but there is no money! Give me a sign." The sign: let someone raise the issue of money. I will take it that you want me to have the house and I will pay the deposit. The particular person whom I presented to the Lord did not raise the issue. That was confirmation. I was forced to turn down the house with some difficulties in that I lost the deposit. The Lord seemed to be answering many of my prayers months after the prayer was made (These prayer requests were made in September 2000). I submit that He was working in His own time. He always comes to our aid on time.

God had spoken. The signs were there to demonstrate that I was not eloping nor escaping my pastoral responsibility to my wife and son. I reflect on the story of David when his brothers had accused him of leaving the sheep to ravenous wolves just to come and spy on the battle between the Israelites and the Philistines. The writer tells us that "Jesse said unto David his son, 'Take now for thy brethren an ephah of this parched corn, and these ten loaves, and run to the camp to thy brethren; And carry these ten cheeses unto the captain of their thousand, and look how thy brethren fare, and take their pledge" (1 Sam.17:17-18). I saw similarities in my own experience. It made me feel as though I was running away from my family. But, my extended stay in the UK was not the case of taking a peep to ascertain what financial and social benefits were there for me. It was not a case of spying out the 'land of opportunity' either. David's trip to the battle-field was undertaken so that his war-trapped brothers could have some extra food. Indeed, his father, Jesse, had sent him on an errand with the nourishing corn and bread for these hungry boys. The father also wanted an urgent, objective, and honest report on the war. This young Israelite boy was always obedient, zealous, fearless and quick to respond.

The writer of 1 Samuel noted that he rose up early the next morning and allowing nothing to hinder him, found someone to look after the family's flock, and dashed for the war zone. After arriving and inquiring of the stakes that were up for grabs, his eldest brother accused him of being proud, espionage, and displaying childish behaviour. Was he out of place to come to watch the war? After all, most boys like to witness action. The young boy had a vision, he had a plan and he was determined based on his response "What have I done? Is there not a cause?" (1 Sam. 17:29). He seemed to be suggesting that he came for a purpose. Ellen White remarks that "by his father's direction he was to carry a message and a gift to his elder brothers and to learn if they were still in safety and health. But, unknown to Jesse, the youthful shepherd had been entrusted with a higher mission. The armies of Israel were in peril, and David had been directed by an angel to save his people."[15] God's people needed help.

I believe firmly that the Lord wanted me to stay for a reason. There was a cause! The Lord had a purpose for me and I was willing to wait until it was revealed and fulfilled. I praise the Lord that I stuck to the mission just as David did. The Lord had provided me with enough evidence to indicate that it was His will that I should be in the UK at the time. How often we find ourselves fighting inner battles about decisions? More profoundly, our outer world can be spiritually depleting, psychologically harsh, and void of any emotional support when we need it most. In such a world, we are faced with discouragements, and we experience torture. These signs that appeared on my journey signalled God's plan for me to stay in the UK and allow His purpose for my life to emerge. It can be the hard way of knowing your purpose in life, but the journey is invaluable.

<u>Taking Time For Reflection</u> {Jot down your thoughts}

- What events have occurred in your life that attempted to shape you?

- How open have you been to the impact of these events?

- What do you think needs to be done with such events?

4
Adopted Son!

"Human beings belong to one great family. The family of God" (*Review and Herald,* June 25, 1908, quoted in White, 1940:*Counsels on Stewardship, p.*24)

In October of 2006 a Pop star and her wealthy husband adopted a one-year-old Malawian boy by the name of David. It was a high-profile adoption. But it was greeted with stormy outbursts and sharp protests from human rights groups scattered across Malawi. The judicial authorities in that African country had waived the local rules and allowed the adoption to proceed. Also the immigration authorities issued little David with the necessary visa and a passport so that he could travel as an emigrant. The way was paved delicately for his imminent departure. Overnight, a small private jet whisked the boy from Lilongwe in Malawi. But an anonymous airport official in Malawi remarked as-a-matter-of-factly that the plane was registered in South Africa and probably headed back to that southern African country. Daily newspapers reports revealed that the little African baby, while on its way to its new British home, was tightly protected by one of the UK pop star's bodyguards and her personal assistant.

They arrived safely at London's Heathrow Airport in the dawn of that Tuesday morning. Little David, whose biological mother died after she gave birth to him, left his distraught father, Yohane, behind in his African birth place. He had swapped unknowingly his home in a dilapidated orphanage near the Zambian border for an extended life of luxury in London with one of the world's most famous couples and their two children. Although, the flight arrived safely at the London's Heathrow Airport, there was speculation that the pop star singer had used her celebrity status to bypass normal adoption rules.[16]

Individuals from various social strata engage in adopting children of varying ages. The reasons for adoption range from the popular view of female infertility to becoming involved in charitable work. Scripture recounts the adoption of Moses: "And the midwives said unto Pharaoh, because the Hebrew women are not as the Egyptian women; for they are lively, and are delivered ere the midwives come in unto them. Therefore God dealt well with the midwives: and the people multiplied, and waxed very mighty. And it came to pass, because the midwives feared God, that he made them houses. And Pharaoh charged all his people, saying, 'Every son that is born ye shall cast into the river, and every daughter ye shall save alive.' And there went a man of the house of Levi, and took to wife a daughter of Levi. And the woman conceived, and bare a son: and when she saw him that he was a goodly child, she hid him three months. And when she could not longer hide him, she took for him an ark of bulrushes, and daubed it with slime and with pitch, and put the child therein; and she laid it in the flags by the river's brink. And his sister stood afar off, to wit what would be done to him. And the daughter of Pharaoh came down to wash herself at the river; and her maidens walked along by the river's side; and when she saw the ark among the flags, she sent her maid to fetch it. And when she had opened it, she saw the child: and, behold, the babe wept. And she had compassion on him, and said, 'This is one of the Hebrews' children'" (Ex 1:19-2:6). It's events like these that we sigh and take deep breaths. We are never sure how the Lord will lead us. They create spiritual tension and suspense. But the author of this pentateuchal book doesn't leave us wondering for too long.

The interaction resumes, "Then said his sister to Pharaoh's daughter, 'Shall I go and call to thee a nurse of the Hebrew women, that she may nurse the child for thee?' And Pharaoh's daughter said to her, 'Go. And the maid went and called the child's mother.' And Pharaoh's daughter said unto her, 'Take this child away, and nurse it for me, and I will give thee thy wages. And the woman took the child, and nursed it.' And the child grew, and she brought him unto Pharaoh's daughter, and he became her son. And she called his name Moses: and she said, 'Because I drew him out of the water' " (Ex.2:7-10). What would become of Moses? What would be his destiny? Only time could have revealed his future. And that's the way it turns out for many of us who experience similar turns in our lives. There can be no fore-knowledge, except with God, because He is all-knowing.

Ellen G. White provides an insightful view of the events regarding Moses' adoption: "The mother's earnest prayers had committed her child to the care of God; and angels, unseen, hovered above his lowly resting place. Angels directed Pharaoh's daughter thither. Her curiosity was excited by the little basket, and as she looked upon the beautiful child within, she read the story at a glance. The tears of the babe awakened her compassion, and her sympathies went out to the unknown mother who had resorted to this means to preserve the life of her precious little one. She determined that he should be saved; she would adopt him as her own. Miriam had been secretly noting every movement; perceiving that the child was tenderly regarded, she ventured nearer....God had heard the mother's prayers; her faith had been rewarded. It was with deep gratitude that she entered upon her now safe and happy task. She felt confident that he had been preserved for some great work, and she knew that he must soon be given up to his royal mother, to be surrounded with influences that would tend to lead him away from God. [17] How do we relate to such event in our own lives? Is it a coincident when events in our lives take an unexpected turn? Is it sheer luck, particularly, on realizing that we were in the right play at the right time? I refer to this as God-incidents, because it's only the God of Heaven that is aware of everything that will occur in our lives. It's His guiding hands that direct our lives along unassumed paths. Without this perspective, we turn a blind eye to the divine involvement in our lives.

In turning to my own experience, life was about to change for me just like it did for these two little helpless babies. How would it come about? I was about to discover the answer? On September 16, 1999, I arrived at the local Seventh-day Adventist church very early that autumn morning. Outside was dark and bleak. It was raining. In the church's court yard, I was greeted by a husband and his wife. They warmly welcomed and eagerly showed me the way into the church. I was the first person after this couple to have arrived at church early. As more people arrived, I felt at home. It was a church full of Caribbean nationals. Those who were close by graciously greeted me. There was a dramatic presentation relating to a biblical character during the morning programme, along with lively inspiring singing and passionate discussions on a biblical text. The singing was melodious. Soloists, groups and the small church choir sang lustily. The preacher for the main service delivered a dynamic sermon. It was powerfully orated. No wonder I felt at home because it reminded me of the church services that are held in many of our churches in the Caribbean.

After the service, the Community Services department hosted a luncheon. Life was about to change for me of which I was unaware. During the afternoon, while everyone was eating the sumptuous meal and fellowshipping amicably with one another, I circled the youth hall energetically, delightfully greeted many people, and boldly introduced myself. The men were dressed in traditional suits, but the women were displaying various fashionable dresses and hats of various colours. Not to mention the coats. The pink dresses, the blue skits, and the lime-coloured blouses illuminated the atmosphere. I noticed a significant number of young people who were sitting cosily together. There was a lot of chatting and laughter. Groups of individuals huddled at their tables to share in the moment and to engage in the conversation of the moment. There was a variety of dishes, but mainly of the Caribbean type. I spotted the mellow sweet-potato pie, the large saucepan of rice and peas, with the steam ascending into the air, the deliciously-looking baked macaroni pie and the well-made salad all laid on the flowered tablecloth. As I orbited the hall, I stumbled upon a family of ten, but only seven were present. They were happy to meet me and on hearing of the country from which I came, that added more joy to their bubbling hearts and smiling faces.

"When did you arrive?" one of the sisters asked.

"I came to the UK on Monday. But I arrived here on Tuesday evening," I replied.

There was a sense of patriotism as I learnt that one of the in-laws was my countryman. What a joy it was to feel at home in a foreign country, particularly when you are surrounded by people of the same culture, background, and national roots!

As I introduced myself to this friendly family, I was startled. Why? The parents, Mr. and Mrs. Searles introduced themselves and each of the five daughters who were present. Mr. Searles was more concerned with his dinner than any thing else. He focused on his meal, but kept an eye on me. Mrs. Searles was very quiet, only offering the passing smile. After each of them was introduced, I shouted:

"All of these? Are there anymore?"

"There are others, but they are not here," a member of the family said.

I was buoying with joy and glee. Immediately, they informed me of the patriotic connections. By this time, Mrs. Searles was more vocal.

"Which country are you from again?" she asked.

"He is from the same country as John, mummy," said one of the daughters.

Since then, my adoption papers were being processed. After lunch, Jean, the oldest of the five daughters that were present (her spouse, John, is my fellow countryman) offered to drive me home. I accepted the offer. As we were driving along, she extended an invitation to her home.

"You can come over to my house sometime next week," she said

"I won't mind," I responded.

"Let me give you a call and confirm which day would be best," said Jean.

"Thank you for that," I replied.

I reached my destination, thanked Jean for the ride and was on my way to my room.

The next Sabbath after worship, Judy, the penultimate daughter of the Searles' family, invited me to their home for lunch.

"Vic, you can come home with us for lunch, today," she informed me.

"Oh! Thank you," I replied.

This is a wonderful, loving, and compassionate family who I firmly believe is guided by the *Hand of God.* I sense their openness to individuals, even though they are a closely knit family. Where would this lead? Was this a one-time event? Was there more invitations to come? He must have been in the centre of their home and actions.

Sometime later, I learnt about the illness of their dad. As an elder in my former home church, among other leadership positions, it was natural for me to visit the sick, so I continued in the same vein as if I were in my previous home church. I visited him on many occasions in hospital. I felt that it was my duty as a fellow-brother to assist in looking after the welfare of a church member. As time elapsed, I intensified my visits both at home and in the hospital with his family's approval. Mr. Searles was a strong individual who upheld right doing and he was not afraid to speak the truth, no matter to whom he was speaking. He expected everyone to behave appropriately, both big and small, and it pleased him when we displayed favourable behaviours. He was a disciplinarian. Misbehaviour never went unnoticed. Besides these characteristics, he was always willing to use his mechanical skills to help others and he showed an interest in the welfare of anyone who visited him. At times, he would say:

"Don't be afraid to ask for anything!"

"Ok," I replied.

The years I spent with him were short, but I thank the Lord for such a man as him because he shared ideas with me, gave advice, and enquired about the welfare of my family. This time made me reminisce on the occasions I spent with my son. I felt as though I belong to this home. I was very relaxed. He showed that he cared by enquiring about my family very often.

"Have you heard from your wife lately? And what about that big fellow?" he would asked.

His love for cricket out-stripped mine, but I found a partner with whom I could watch test and one-day cricket matches whenever possible. Whenever I visited I would stay with him and watch whatever cricket match was showing. At times we were disgruntled about the players' performance. We clapped. We shouted. We criticised. We were pundits on the game. We had something in common and this helped to tighten the bond between us. I was also encouraged to come to the house more frequently. This was in response to Judy who had extended this invitation by saying that the doors were opened. *What did I do to deserve this? Nothing of which I can think!*

As my studies progressed rapidly, I was invited to other cultural activities by other individuals of similar nationality to mine. I attended events such as concerts and my country's Annual Overseas Independence Day services. My first concert was thrilling, in that I was ecstatic to be out with my fellow-country folk and with those of similar moral and spiritual values. The concerts reminded me of some of the ones I attended when I was in my home country. Thrilling voices. Familiar lyrics. Inspiring words. Sensational music. The Independence Day church service was one of a kind. It was a socio-cultural event where I met some of the senior folk from my home country. In chatting with many of them, I discovered that many of them migrated thirty, forty and fifty years before my arrival to the UK. These moments were historical. The older folks shared some of their early experiences with me such as the harsh winter conditions, the small wages they worked for, and the meagre accommodation they obtained. I also came into contact with fellow university students, some of whom lived in the same accommodation as I at the time. Wow! These were exciting evenings. I was thrilled to be among such individuals. It provided me with an opportunity to socialise outside the university setting. Being in the company of individuals of a similar cultural background comforted me greatly. We reminisced with each other, sharing common thoughts about politics, state of affairs in our home country, linguistic idioms and national sayings. From these events, I was able to link up with other friends who I could visit and with whom I could go on trips.

The interaction between the Searles family and I continued. Soon I became aware that there were difficult moments for this family, but with much prayer, the mighty *Hand of God* kept their dad alive and strong while he battled the illness. The Divine Hand moved over and comforted everyone. He soothed their hearts and consoled them during these moments of pain. I would visit at least once a week and give whatever support I could. This family endured trying moments. They were often going back and forth to the hospital. It was physically and emotionally draining. Many times they would have to rush from work or school to visit dad at hospital. The sleep was weighing down on their eyes. The tiredness was visible on their weary faces.

Up until this time, I still referred to Mrs. Searles as Sister Searles. One day, Judy and I were chatting about a church matter. In her conversation, she said: "Just as we have adopted you…" For a few days, that word 'adopted' rested on my mind and many thoughts flowed through my head. *Adopted! Have they adopted me?* I asked myself. I did not have the faintest idea that they did. I felt very welcome among them.

In retrospect, the invitations to their home, the lunch invitations, the welcomes, and the telephone calls had been signalling this rapidly, but, somehow, I was too blind to notice it. This wonderful treatment towards me was written in concrete and only a blind man would miss it. As time elapsed, this family made me feel more and more welcomed. They called my home regularly to enquire about my well-being and such calls were also reciprocated.

I mustered the courage and one day, in referring to Mrs. Searles, I said, "Mum." It was strange at first. I was shock initially. In my mind I wondered, *how would she respond? How would she react? What would she do?* Her response was far from my apprehensions. It was an embracing one. Daily she became my mum and her children became my siblings. The children in this family and I interacted as brothers and sisters. The opportunity to have siblings was an experience that I had always longed for, especially while I was growing up. I was consciously aware of these adopted siblings in my life. Mum worked tirelessly in the nursing profession and was eager to ensure that her children had a Christian experience, even though each of them made his/her own choices.

This family supported me throughout the completion of my postgraduate studies. I was and am still grateful for the untiring support they gave me, especially when I had to stay overnight on many occasions in the university's computer room for four weeks (except during Sabbath hours) to complete my dissertation. They gave me advice on many issues such as getting work, how to make telephone calls to my family, and where to shop. They shared ideas with me, and ensured that I was doing well by God's grace. It was their caring nature, the prayers of Maria (my wife), Josiah (my son), friends and the grace of God that carried me through the tough times.

I thanked my Father moment by moment for this family to whom I brought my plans and ideas. Their home was a place where I found comfort and friendship. It was a place where my sorrows were cushioned and where I found happiness.

The psychological impact of adoption on individuals tends to emerge. Research conducted by Child Welfare Information Gateway indicates that, along with the issues of identity are issues of self-esteem. The researchers believe that adopted individuals often score lower on measures of self-esteem and self-confidence. This result may reflect the fact that some adopted persons may view themselves as different, out-of-place, unwelcome, or rejected. Some of these feelings may result from the initial loss of birth parents and from growing up away from siblings, and extended family members.[18] Was I experiencing these psychological traits? It may have been, but with the passage of time, I overcame the negative effects. At such times, we have a sense of belonging. In such close-knit families who reach out to us, it is here that such a need can be met. It's the human heart that yearns for it. We are never made to be in our own cocoon. I was thrilled to have Sis. Searles, Jean, Judy, and Mel at my side during the graduation for my Master's. It was a memorable occasion. They were my family away from my family. They all congratulated me for a well-earned achievement and indeed I deserved it after all the sleepless nights and the inconveniences which I had to endure.

Indeed, my Father has brought me into a family whom I grew to love, appreciate, and respect. A hidden place is in my heart for every member of this family. I do not believe that I performed any special feat to become an adopted son. It was divinely planned. As I commune with the Lord, I carry each member of this family frequently to God's Throne, requesting that He would keep them near the cross, surround them with

His Spirit and give them grace to follow and serve Him. There is no doubt that I felt the Hand of God during this phase of my studies. He was not only moulding and preparing me for a task ahead, but he was preparing me to be part of a family that He created to carry out His mission.

Taking Time For Reflection [Jot down your thoughts]

- Who is there for you when you feel as though you are in a world by yourself?

- Look around and think back carefully. There has been someone trying to reach out to you. How have you been responding to that person?

- Would you be willing to give up some of your time to help that other person in time of need?

5
Everlasting Trials?

"Trial is part of the education given in the school of Christ, to purify God's children from the dross of earthliness. It is because God is leading His children that trying experiences come to them. Trials and obstacles are His chosen methods of discipleship and His appointed conditions of success" (White, *Acts of the Apostles*: 524)

The Apostolic group had begun to spread the gospel, first, in their home cities and later, in other places. They were of one mind, they fellowshipped together, thus, allowing friendships to develop and drowning out partiality and selfishness. As they began to rejoice and praise the Lord for His miraculous performance on the Day of Pentecost, sadness began to fill the air. Did they bargain for sorrow, disappointments, or opposition? How were they to handle the religious, social, and political strife that were to surface?

Reflecting on the era of Jesus' disciples, the writer of Acts of the Apostles tells us that the religious leaders and sectarian groups of the time began to pester and persecute God's messengers by threatening them with imprisonment and beatings if they had continued to preach or teach about Jesus and His resurrection. But, while this was occurring, those who had heard the message of salvation, believed in Jesus, thus causing the number of believers to swell by thousands. Luke, the writer of the book of Acts, tells us that "As they spoke to the people, the priests, the captain of the temple, and the Sadducees came upon them, being greatly disturbed that they taught the people and preached in Jesus the resurrection from the dead. And they laid hands on them, and put *them* [sic] in custody until the next day, for it was already evening. However, many of those who heard the word believed; and the number of the men came to be about five thousand" (Acts 4:1-3, NKJV). Was not this the saving power of God at work? What does this situation tell us about God? It seems to confirm that nothing can stop his message of salvation from reaching the minds of individuals. Isaiah, under the inspiration of the Spirit of God, writes: "...my word...shall not return unto me void, but it shall accomplish that which I please, and it shall prosper in the thing whereto I sent it" (55:11). Often times it may appear as though the adversary is winning, but God always has the last say and brings us out to be more than conquerors so that His name may be praised and be glorified. This religious conflict did not hinder God's mission. As the religious leaders of the day congregated and plotted to disturb the disciples, the Holy Spirit spoke explicitly through Peter with words that cut to the heart. This ushered in the beginning of everlasting trials for the people of that era who were on God's mission.

Looking back, I accepted the fact that God knows best and that if it is His will, all that I prayed for will be granted. The prayer and fasting sessions had changed drastically to the extent that my prayer list was shortened to seven items. I needed to be kept focus. I yearned for a new experience and I also felt the need to be empowered. I also wanted to experience the power of God in my life. There was a need to rise to a higher spiritual level seeing that there was a need for direction in my life. There was a deep longing to know and hear the voice of God. I did not want to drift along with the everyday tides and currents because I believe that there is something more than the hum-drum of daily living. I came to a point where I began asking the God of Heaven what was going on in my life and why he was allowing all of these situations to occur. It's when our backs are against a wall and we are locked in with no room to turn that we gain a new perspective and see the bigger picture.

As I studied St. Luke 12, the Holy Spirit made me understand that worrying is useless, from the perspective that he will continue to look after me. As I write at this moment under the inspiration of the Holy Spirit, Psalm 127:2 comes to mind, thus reiterating Luke 12 to the point that it is a waste of time worrying about our cares and problems, for indeed, He [Jesus] gives His beloved children ample sleep. Moreover, the words of Jeremiah, the prophet: "Do not be afraid of the king of Babylon, whom you now fear. Do not be afraid of him, declares the LORD, for I am with you and will save you and deliver you from his hands" (42:11, NIV) particularly consolidated God's intentions: it was through this that I recognised the importance of being obedient to his plan and guidance.

It was during these months that I was also battling with the Ministry of Education to grant me study leave to pursue the doctoral programme and also to defer my bonded service. Within two months, I was granted the deferral of bonded service, which meant that I did not have to repay my scholarship through the form of employment until after three years. Oh what a wonderful God we serve! It was a long and hard battle. I had to write numerous letters requesting leave and responding to the Ministry of Education because of the threat of firing me. It cost me tears, sleepless nights which I spent on my knees agonising with the God of the universe and it cost me my teaching job from which I resigned. There was no study leave, but this deferral coincided with my visa. Both were for three years. I was relieved convincingly. I accepted this situation. What was God's purpose in granting this amount of time? I am yet to discover! When we take a look at our circumstances, we can conclude that there are many things we just don't understand. The human mind is finite and for God to pull back the curtains of time and give us a peep into the future, we would probably sink beneath the earth because of what is ahead for us. Ellen G. White remarks that "There are times when it seems to the servant of God impossible to do the work necessary to be done, because of the lack of means to carry on a strong, solid work. But if they advance in faith, the salvation of God will be revealed, and prosperity will attend their efforts. In the upbuilding [sic] of His work the Lord does not always make everything plain before His servants. He sometimes tries the confidence of His people by bringing about circumstances which compel them to move forward in faith. Often He brings them into strait and trying places, and bids them advance when their feet seem to be touching the waters of Jordan. It is at such times, when the prayers of His servants ascend to Him in earnest faith, that God opens the way before them and brings them out into a large place. When God's messengers recognize their responsibilities toward the needy portions of the Lord's vineyard, and in the spirit of the Master Worker labor [sic] untiringly for the conversion of souls, the angels of God will prepare the way before them, and the means necessary for the carrying forward of the work will be provided."[19] Our trials at times are difficult and arduous. We are never sure where to turn and that's why the writer of in the book of Hebrews reminds us that "Without faith it is impossible to please him:

for he that cometh to God must believe that he is, and that he is a rewarder of them that diligently seek him" (11:6).

The first Youth Day in 2001 was a day I would never forget. The entire day's programme was directed by the youth. We presented the morning programme by including invigorating gospel music and heated discussions on a very topical subject. Some of the young people were also ushers for the day. As assistant youth leader, I was asked to lead the mid-say service. The sermon for the mid-day service that [Saturday] Sabbath day was delivered by a dynamic guest speaker. He was tall, burly, muscular, and had a deep bass voice. He was vibrant in the pulpit. As he spoke, I felt that the Lord was instructing me to give up the doctoral programme. In the sermon, he focused on Abraham's test with Isaac. I reasoned with this impression and came up with the view that since the Lord had allowed me to be accepted for the programme, I could not see it possible for him to be saying this to me six months after I was enrolled on the course at the university. I wrestled sorrowfully with the decision for a long, long, long time. I felt very uncomfortable. There was a fear that overwhelmed me. From previous experiences, I knew that this air of fear surrounding me was the Holy Spirit impressing on me to abandon the doctoral studies. This emotional feeling was not producing negative effects. I felt afraid to carry out this deed. *Was this God telling me to pull out of the programme or my own thoughts? What would happen if I don't?* I thought to myself. This was where the fear had originated.

After the mid-day service, the youth team held a luncheon in the youth hall for everyone. There were scores of people waiting in the long queue to be served. The odour and aroma from the kitchen almost filled me. What I saw displayed on the table was mouth-watering. It looked tasty and appetising. More and more dishes were brought out. Even the steam from the piping-hot food carried the appetising odour into the atmosphere. During this time, I mentioned my inner convictions to a few people. I was deeply troubled. I needed someone to talk to then. Coincidentally or by divine intervention, Mel, the last daughter of the Searles' family, was standing in front of me.

"I feel as though I am going to give up the doctorate," I said softly.

"Why?", she inquired surprisingly.

"I was impressed today to give it up," I replied in a pensive mood.

"That's not like you. What cause you to change your mind?" she queried.

"I just feel that is how the Lord is leading me," I added.

"Give it some time. Probably you are tired and have too much going on now," she advised.

"Yep. True. Probably you are right," I remarked.

Although I had prayed for a new experience, I never in my wildest dreams envisaged that the Lord would allow me to become bankrupt one month after that prayer. My philosophy up to this time seemed to have been shaping my goal and purpose in life. It seemed as though I was acting independently of the Holy Spirit and God. This appeared paradoxical to me. On the one hand, I was eager to carry out the mission that the Lord had lay on my heart, but on the other hand, I was very keen to pursue my own dream and goals, by chasing after a doctoral degree. McMinn reminds us that "the consequences of unbounded independence are woundedness, brokenness and pain....And as we see throughout the Old Testament, a nation [*or individual*] that turns away from God faces pain and loss. Eventually the myth of self-sufficiency sours, and we are left staring at our neediness, confronted with the brokenness and pain that have shadowed independence throughout human history. Sometimes pain is caused by personal rebellion."[20] As I reflect on all that was transpiring in my life: the lack of funds for my studies, losing the house deposit, the denial of study leave, and the resignation from teaching, these inevitable events were signalling to me that I was ignoring the voice of the Holy Spirit. I appeared to be obedient, but in reality, I was becoming self-reliant.

The university had taken its fees out of my bank account which only had three hundred pounds at the time. By this time I was in the red by twenty-four hundred pounds. I hadn't gotten over the enormity of this problem before the bank could write to me about this heightened financial mountain. Bankruptcy! The financial adviser informed in no uncertain terms that I would have to repay the debt in twenty-eight days and that I could not have access to my weekly wages. *Why did this happen? Why did God allow this shattering experience to come? How would I get out of this? Is this the beginning of the time of trouble?* I asked myself. My mind raced swiftly to the prophetic teachings about the end of time that my denomination expounds. *Is this the time when we would be unable to buy or sell unless we possess the mark of the beast?* It certainly was for me! In essence, I had no access to money although I was working weekly. I was devastated, shocked, shaken and in disbelief. My whole life stood still. I could not buy anything. It was even too expensive to purchase a stamp for twenty-two pence. I could not even write my wife and son. I felt like a pauper. McMinn reminds us that "brokenness is a prerequisite to understanding God's grace, but the Christian Gospel does not leave us in a state of broken despair."[21] Slowly, I did come to this realisation. There was no money for transportation, which meant that I could not travel to work or do anything else. I became radical in my prayer by questioning my Father: "Lord, what are you saying to me?" I needed answers to my spiritual dilemma and the woes that crept into my life. I longed for a divine response.

One morning, I took a bus into the North Yorkshire city of Harrogate on my way to school. It was an express bus and would only stop at selected locations. The bus raced along the partially busy dual carriageway as the cold wind beat against its body. There were more workers disembarking than embarking. As the bus was speeding along, I surveyed the agricultural fields which spread over a large lush expanse of land. Corn. Strawberries. Carrots. The residents' in this area had some flower gardens that were beautifully decorated and well manicured. I reached the bus station on time, but as I boarded a bus to travel to the school, the bus driver told me in no uncertain terms that I could not use my bus pass because this was North Yorkshire and mine was for West Yorkshire.

"But I came up on it!"

"Well you shouldn't have, and you will need to pay."

"I don't have any money. What am I going to do?"

"You will have to get off the bus."

"How far is the school?" I probed.

"Five minutes around the corner. You can walk."

Wow! For me, this was divinely orchestrated. I jumped off the bus and trodded briskly down the cobbler stone street, looking out every few paces for this school. In my mind, I was wondering how I would get back home. I quickly came to the conclusion that I would take the train in the afternoon.

School eventually came to an end and I rushed out into the hot glistening summer sun to catch an early train. I was of the opinion that I could use the pass on the train. This famous bus pass can be used either on the bus or the train. I jumped on a train that was westbound, sat in a double seat and made myself comfortable. Within a few minutes, a stately looking conductor approached me and repeated the usual phrase, "tickets please!" He held the ticket punch in one hand and had the ticket machine hung around his neck. It looked heavy. I could see the strain on his neck. On his left shoulder was his conductor's cash bag. I took out my bus pass. To my amazement, as the train hurriedly raced along the tracks, the business-like conductor replied, "That can't work."

"Why?" I asked.

"It is out of the zone. This is north."

"So what must I do," I replied. "I don't have any money."

"Well, you'll have to get off at the next stop."

I would have had to pay the fare for four stops before my pass could be acceptable. This fare was about three pounds. The panic button went off. I quickly pushed my hands into my coat pocket, took out my cards, and gave the conductor my debit card with the words: "See if that works." The evening sunlight was streaming through the transparent train window. It was hot and bright. The sky was blue and clear as crystal. A few odd birds flew overhead. He punched in the account numbers as I waited patiently. Out came the pink and white perforated ticket. Praise the Lord! I thank the Mighty God for bringing me through this one. But it cost me. The bank charged me twenty-five pounds for using the card, seeing that I was already too high in my overdraft.

On another occasion, I took a bus into East Yorkshire. It was an extremely sunny day and as I travelled briskly through a small town there, I was caught in the hustle and bustle of the morning. Cars were speeding along the carriageway, pedestrians, looking stern and in a concentrating mood, were whisking their way to their destinations. I left one bus and entered another, expecting to be ferried off to school within a few minutes. Astonishingly, my bus pass did not cover the zone in which I was going. I had to disembark. As I stepped off the bus, the driver pondered. I was desperate in my heart because I was late for work and had to go. That huge debt had to be repaid. He asked me how much money I had. I told him that I had twenty pence, to which he responded that he could not take me because he did not have a fare for that amount of money. Sounding eager to take me, he explained,

"If I put you on the bus and the inspectors come and find you with a twenty-pence ticket, my job is on the line. I can't help you."

Immediately, a kind young lady who was standing in the background, near the bus stop, asked, "Don't you have enough fare?"

I turned around. She was short, slim and was carrying a handbag.

"No," I replied.

She further probed to find out how much I needed and I told her that I needed a pound. Out came the brazen cylindrical coin. I expressed sincere gratitude, jumped on the bus, paid the fare, and sat with thanksgiving in my heart and on my lips. Who was she? Where did she come from? What was she doing there? How did she know that I did not have any money? I was lost for answers. The bus drove off. Was my Father in this situation? Were the angels and the Spirit of God moving upon these two persons? I have no doubt that the answer to these questions is yes.

It was a Tuesday morning, in the peak of summer 2001, when the teaching agency, for which I worked at the time, assigned me to a school near my home. I only had ninety pence in my pocket that day and I thought to myself, *I will walk to work!* I had come to this decision because I did not want to spend the only money I had to my name. However, in my mind, I reasoned that if I decided to walk, I may reach the school late. I was also of the view that the fare to the school would only be sixty pence. Punctuality was the driving force for the teaching agency, so I decided to take a bus. To my amazement, when I boarded the bus and told the driver where I was going, he said, "Ninety pence." *Oh! No!* I sighed to myself. I walked reluctantly to my seat, slumped into the seat dejectedly and immediately decided that I would walk home in the evening seeing that I had no more money, now or in the foreseeable future, so I thought.

I disembarked the bus and was making my way up the street where the school was located. It was quiet. There were still many cars parked on both sides of the street. It looked as if no human being had risen from the previous night sleep. There was no sign of anyone. There was a calm breeze and the chilly morning breeze was bearable. I saw stream of cars still parked in their space. As I came closer to the stationary cars on my right hand side, I saw some silver coins near the front tyre of a car. As I reached that spot, I bent down and there, three coins confronted me: a fifty pence and two twenty pence all sitting strategically on top of each other. I was moved by this, and after picking them up, I uttered a word of thanks, shook my head, and continued on to the school. It was miraculous and beyond my imagination. It was awesome! Did a passer-by drop those coins in such a uniformed manner the night before or so early in the morning? Or did my Heavenly Father, who knew my needs, placed them there for me? I have no doubt that He did.

The book of Jonah depicts a similar story to mine. In response to the divine command to denounce the ungodly lifestyle of the Ninevites, the writes states that "Jonah arose to flee to Tarshish from the presence of the Lord. He went down to Joppa, and found a ship going to Tarshish; so he paid the fare, and went down into it, to go with them to Tarshish from the presence of the Lord. But the Lord sent out a great wind on the sea, and there was a mighty tempest on the sea so that the ship was about to be broken" (Jonah 1:3-4, NKJV). Was I displaying tendencies similar to those of Jonah in diverting from the real purpose of being in the UK? Was I clinging on to my academic goals that would only lead me down to 'Tarshish' when the Lord wanted me to go to 'Nineveh'? It seemed that these perils were "hair-raising phenomena"[22] which the Lord was using to pursue me and attract my attention.

I could not wait for the next weekend when I would engage in another prayer and fasting session because I wanted to know what to do. I wanted to know where I was going wrong and what He was saying to me. Through the Spirit of God, I focussed on the Holy Scripture and the Lord made me aware of four principles: The Moses, Abraham, David, and Gideon principles. God had given Abraham a son and He asked him back for his son in the form of a sacrifice. Did God really want Abraham to slaughter Isaac? Was Abraham going to carry out the act seriously? Yes! For me, the Lord was saying to give up the doctoral studies, but I unlike Abraham, rationalized this request and said that God would not give me something and then take it away from me. It could have been a conflict of wills, but I was still not convinced that it was the correct decision. I was of the view that I could pull through by God's grace and come out victoriously.

In my valley and deep pit, I prayed in line with the Moses principle asking the Lord to deliver me from this financial yoke, otherwise the people around would mock and speculate about my spiritual sincerity. As David planned to fight against the mighty Philistines, he asked the Lord whether he should go or not. I did the same. The fourth time David asked the Lord for the time scale in which to attack the enemy, the Lord told him to plan an ambush, but only move when he heard the top of the mulberry bush making a noise. *Lord, what is my 'mulberry bush'?* I asked. I decided that the outcome of my two assignments would put the nail in the coffin, allowing me to pack up and return permanently to my family in the Caribbean.

It came to a point where I had to rise and act. Like Jehosophat, I was weak because the situation was more than I could bear, I thought. I did not know how to wriggle out of the situation, but my eyes were fixed firmly upon the Lord (2 Chronicles 20:12). I refrained from calling the banking centre for fear of what they would tell me. I rose in the power of the Spirit of God one afternoon and dialled the number. I was unsuccessful in making contact for some time. Soon after, success came and I eventually spoke with an advisor who helped me to set up a budget. Finally, after interrogating me about the reasons for the mountainous overdraft, she agreed to set my overdraft limit at a specific level that should not be exceeded monthly. I had three months to get rid of my twenty-four hundred problems, but it incurred some interest. I praised the Lord as my family and friends came to my rescue because, although there was money, it was unable to offset all of the bills with which I was plagued. On many occasions, my friends brought groceries, gave small amounts of cash, prayed with and for me and also called to inquire about my well-being.

During the final prayer and fasting session, the Spirit of God had placed me in a pensive mood, while I was walking circumspectly and waiting for my mulberry bush to make a noise. By this time, I was asking the Lord whether the mission of mentoring the youth was over and whether I should return home to the Caribbean permanently. I came to realize that, as children of the Light, we need to plan through prayer and so I decided mentally to continue my studies from at home. There can be no escaping from some situations and so the grades were important. They would decide the outcome of my doctoral programme here in the United Kingdom, so I thought.

Having not received my results in my student mailbox, I strolled over to my department's office and inquired about my results. The secretary, being surprised that I had not received my results, marched over to the filing cabinet, hastily pulled out the middle drawer and leafed through some files. She pulled out my result sheet, looked at it and shook her head. Immediately I sensed that something was not right. I was praying in my heart. She slowly took out a brown official envelope, placed the results in it and sealed the flap. A feeling overshadowed me on the spot. I took the envelope from her and sauntered down the flight of stairs. I left the office praying: "Lord you know that I prayed and fasted over these assignments. You know I needed a B-grade". As I was opening the envelope, my hands shook with fright. I was tense. When my eyes lighted upon the grade C+, my heart sunk. I was pensive. It was nerve-racking and incredible. *Lord what are you saying? Should I go back to the Caribbean?* I thought to myself. That C+ grade was fifty-nine percent. I felt the Lord was saying to me 'thus far and no further.' How could a person be given fifty-nine percent for an essay when that was only one mark short of sixty percent? The results for the second assignment were worse: (Grade D). That was it! I booked my flight and began contacting the university in my country to request information about the doctoral programme in educational psychology.

Additionally, I had no intentions of going back into the primary school classroom if I had returned to the Caribbean.

Therefore, I decided to make enquiries about vacancies at the university in my home country. Was I losing focus of the mission? Or was it that the Lord was waiting patiently on me to obey his promptings? How do such trials assist us in our spiritual walk with the Lord? They provide us with inner strength and they also help us to face other difficulties. E White provides a spiritual perspective to such occurrences by noting that "The trials of life are God's workmen, to remove the impurities and roughness from our characters. Their hewing, squaring, and chiselling, their burnishing and polishing, is a painful process, it is hard to be pressed down to the grinding wheel. But the stone is brought forth prepared to fill its place in the heavenly temple. Upon no useless material does the Master bestow such careful, thorough work. Only His precious stones are polished after the similitude of a palace."[23] The Lord also kept me focused on Him, and I was willing to discover His ultimate goal for my life. I walked circumspectly and soberly. There was no time to waste, and I longed to obey and respond to my Lord's guidance. In hindsight, there seemed to be a parallel between young Samuel's call and mine experience in that both of us "did not yet know the Lord" (1 Sam 3:7). Indeed, they felt like everlasting trials, but, the Lord delivered me. I thank Him even now for his everlasting mercies which are renewed daily.

One thing was certain. The "dogged persistence of God"[24] was evident in my life and I believe that He went after me like He did with Jonah to ensure that His Will was accomplished in my life. I could only confess that these trials and storms were instigated divinely and they echoed the unchanging nature of the Almighty and Omniscient God.

My financial collapse demonstrates that, as humans, we get out of control and can never get it right. No amount of fighting, struggling, or rationalisation solves the heart issue. There is a pull within us. But God urges us to surrender to Him so that He can transform us into the unique person He desires us to be. We can never see what's up ahead because it's a path travelled by faith. But, even more, it's about coming to the realization that you are needed to help humanity find its rightful place in the divine scheme of events. I call this having a vision to be that special individual in God. Who are you now? Who will you be in five years? While this perspective never dawned on me before, it's this kind of thinking that needs to be part of our mental process.

Taking Time For Reflection [Jot down your thoughts]

- If you have had any adverse circumstances, how have they shaped you afterwards?

- What resources have you used to assist you during those trying times?

- What thoughts ran through your mind during your ordeal?

- What have you been running away from?

- Why do you think you have taken this route?

6
Moments of Agony

"For His anger endureth for a moment; in His favour is life: weeping may endure for a night, but joy cometh in the morning" (Ps 30:5, KJV)

Over the years, the Lord has blessed me with patience and imparted inner strength, courage, and faith, all of which, along with much prayer, carried me through many ordeals. Although my family travelled on many occasions, there was never a moment that I missed them to the point of tears. Moreover, I was surrounded by the familiar: family, relatives, colleagues, and Christian friends. When we consider the significance of having familiar elements in our lives, we experience comfort, peace of mind, emotional strength, and we gain the courage to be free and open. Psychologically, the familiar elements around us satisfy the need for belonging and love, a higher order need that every individual longs to satisfy. This was about to change as I began experiencing painful moments of agony.

During my first autumn in the UK, my course group in my university department was invited to a technology exhibition in Doncaster, a Southern Yorkshire town. There were ten students on my course: nine females and one male. Most of these students were from Greece, one was from Cyprus and the other was a Lebanese. The group and I journeyed by train and taxi. As we sat together in the train, the girls were chatting with each other. There was much laughter and smiles emanating from them. The topic seemed to be of mutual interest for them to be enthused and be fascinated by the discussion. There were hardly any verbal exchanges between them and myself. But Maria, one of the Greek students, occasionally looked up and asked:

"Are you ok, Victor?

"Yep, I am alright, just relaxing," I replied casually on one occasion.

After arriving at the train station, we headed for a taxi because we did not want to arrive late for the exhibition. It was at this time, that I felt a sense of loneliness. I felt cut off from my outer world. It was a case of being in a crowd, among scores of people, but yet lonely. I seemed to be lost in the midst of a busy and hectic town. We arrived at the busy conference centre. There were hundreds of attendants. We admired and observed various pieces of equipment for people with learning disabilities: loop system, computer-aided telephones among others. We also perused different kinds of books and other teaching materials that would be beneficial to people with learning disabilities. Within twenty minutes of looking around, something overpowered me and tears flowed down my cheeks like a burst pipe. Maria, my Greek classmate, came over and tried to console me.

"What's wrong, Victor?" she asked.

My tears continued to flow.

"Do you want to tell me?" she pressed.

By this time, one of the other students had alerted our tutor, Sue. She was a caring, genuine, and considerate individual. She quickly came over, hugged me, and was wading her way into my thoughts to bring me to myself.

"Are you missing your family?" she queried.

"Is your son still coming over to the UK?"

Sometime prior to attending the exhibition I had told my class that Josiah, my son, would have been joining me for the Christmas holiday. She took me away from the centre of action, in an obscure area, where very little activities were taking place. Her assistance calmed me down. I resumed my viewing of the equipment and materials which were on display.

My moment of agony seemed to have emerged from the culture of individualism that prevailed in my department. Gary Collin points out that "Lonely people appear in all vocational groups, but there is evidence that highly ambitious, 'fast-track', upwardly mobile people (including the much discussed yuppies and baby boomers) have an especially high incidence of loneliness.[25] Could I have been experience hidden loneliness and was unaware of it? It seemed that way. Collins further notes that "Loneliness is the painful awareness that we lack close and meaningful contact with others. It involves a feeling of inner emptiness, isolation, and intense longing. Even when they are surrounded by others, lonely people often feel left out, unwanted, rejected, or misunderstood. Frequently, there are feelings of sadness, discouragement, restlessness, and anxiety, accompanied by a longing to be wanted and needed by at least one human being."[26] How do you cope with times of loneliness? What do you do when you see knitted family and friends engaging in activities that you long to do with your own family? On the conscious level of my mind, I was keen on pursuing my studies, however, on the sub-conscious level, I was lonely. Psychologically, prolonged deprivation of the need for belonging and love overtakes us. It leads to a feeling of rejection or loneliness. That was the answer. Loneliness! This loneliness attacked me on many occasions and anywhere: in church, in my room and in the library. I would weep bitterly, almost uncontrollably, until I regain my composure. As time elapsed, my tear ducts worked extremely hard. I was touched by many events.

Sometime in the autumn of 2000, I needed to complete registration for the doctoral programme. The registration documents were sent to me from my department, but I did not have a penny. By this time, my family, friends, and I were praying desperately for God to come through for me. This financial situation seemed to overwhelm me. It was unbearable. One morning during devotions, as I reached out to the Lord in prayer about the matter, I wept bitterly and incessantly. I screamed and pleaded to Him with a heavy heart. I was broken. Life seemed so harsh and difficult. There seemed to be no light at the end of my journey. But I saw the mercies of the Lord that morning. He impressed on Judy to call me the same time. We had planned to meet for prayer, but the time was not arranged. I was at my wits end and in tears. She was so touched that she prayed earnestly for me over the telephone. I had never heard her pray like that before nor since. She assured me that she would come over so that we could spend some time in prayer and bible study. That time of prayer provided comfort and helped me to keep focus, with the understanding that the Lord will come through. The text that gave me extra hope is Psalm 30:5. It has been an inspiration for me knowing that "…weeping may endure for a night, but joy cometh in the morning." During my desert experiences, I have been reassured that, one day, my Father will respond to my pleas.

Whenever we pray with a sincere heart for new experiences, it is certain that the Lord will respond. Some of the questions we need to ask ourselves are: Am I ready for a new experience? What will I do when God opens the flood gates of trials or draw me to my 'cross'? How will I respond if it seems that God is absent during these difficult moments? What will be my resolve if God puts me on hold for a while? Can I handle the silent treatment from Heaven that may come my way? In hindsight, I discover that there were times when I did not handle a new experience well. As I sense the need for a new upward spiritual move, I not only asked for a new experience, but also for the wisdom to handle the new experience. It's about being specific in prayer and praying with wisdom through the Holy Spirit.

The year 2001 was very eventful because there were many devastating moments of agony for me. Many months, both day and night were littered with tears, agony and pain. In the early part of the year, I was teaching the Junior Power Point Sabbath School class. The children in this class were between 12 and 14 years of age. They had different personalities and learning styles. And so, I would use various strategies to teach the bible lesson. I used puzzles, quizzes and role play. The classroom we used was partially decorated. A plant was here and there, along with a few drawings on the wall. There were few chairs and an old tattered flowered carpet that covered the creaking floor. That morning, as we began to delve into the lesson, two of the students hurled a barrage of questions at me. I tried to answer them, but the more I provided a response, the deeper the questions were becoming.

"Where does God come from?" one of the female students asked.

"And why does he allow all these bad things to happen to people, if he says that he is God?" the other female student added.

One of my male students asked, "Why do we have to come to church?"

What was this all about? What were they trying to achieve by asking all of these debatable questions? I pondered. My 'melting pot' was full of spiritual issues and circumstances. On the surface, I was kept in tact by God's grace and strength. However, in my inner being, there were spiritual battles that I was fighting. I was struggling with many of life's complex issues: No scholarship, difficulties with obtaining study leave and missing my family. I found it hard to come to grips with. What am I doing that I shouldn't be doing? Where should I really be? I wrestled painfully with such questions.

This episode caused my emotional cup to overflow, not with joy, but with pain. I broke down in tears, weeping uncontrollably and incessantly. No amount of comfort from my assistant children division leaders would help. They hugged me and patted me on the back to calm me. I knew they were present, but I was in another world, overcome by sorrow, hurt, and pain. The midday service came and went. But I remained riveted to the seat where I was sitting since 10 o'clock that Sabbath morning. As time faded away, I composed myself, but a pensive mood gripped me. I was very quiet and hardly spoke. I spent that Sabbath day and the proceeding week walking circumspectly and in a very contemplative mood.

As time went on, I found myself longing for the young people in the church where I was worshipping to excel. They were enthusiastic, closely knitted and had a desire for evangelism. This zeal was often expressed in a variety of ways such as conducting our own prayer and fast sessions and bible study. The last youth day for the year 2001 was a testing one for many of us in that the youth department had encouraged back—to-back preaching during the mid-day Sabbath (Saturday) service.

Five of the young ladies were asked to deliver a sermonette for ten minutes each that morning. The Holy Spirit moved on them. As they ministered, I surveyed them and perceived potential in God's children with whom I was working. They spoke vivaciously with passion and vitality. Judy, my adopted sister, was the last preacher and as she spoke on the topic 'the prodigal girl', her message was interspersed with tears. The atmosphere was calm. There was a hush. My heart longed to see her totally surrendered. I longed for the Lord to bring her around. It pained me to see that, although they were eager and inspired, it seemed that they were not ready to go all the way with their Redeemer and surrender their all to him. I could not hold back the tears. It was another painful moment of agony. I was overpowered. I was stuck to my seat. Even after the service had ended and the congregation was leaving, I was still unmoved. Some of my friends remained with me. They hugged me. Others patted me on the back. Some of the brethren spoke of the working of the Holy Spirit in my life, others muttered inaudibly, a few passed by and acknowledged my pain, while others gave words of comfort during my time of agony.

Very often, we tend to portray a strong mentality and an emotionally stable personality. Nevertheless, as we delve into the inner thoughts, many profound issues begin to surface. For me, there were many issues that continued to stare me in the face to the extent that I could not bring an end to them. I had to wait until the Lord was finished moulding me for His task.

One cold morning after an inspired devotional session, I rushed to catch a bus to go to work. I interspersed the brisk walking with running. I reached the bus stop, embarked the bus and was very relieved to get a seat. I was still panting. My heart was racing. I sat in the upper deck of the bus which was partially empty. It was raining lightly. The rain water from the bus' roof trickled down its side. Immediately after sitting, I burst into a river of tears. I felt overwhelmed. What went wrong at that moment? I do not know. I took out my cellular phone and sent a few SOS text messages to my friends, asking them to pray for me. I am reminded very often of the Psalmist who asked the Lord to hear his cry so that "when my heart is overwhelmed: lead me to the rock that is higher than I" (Ps.61:2). But on this occasion, I needed human ears, hands and shoulders. What a painful morning that was! Just sitting there on the upper deck of a bus early in the morning, with tears flowing down my cheeks and I simply could not stop them.

I praise my Redeemer and Saviour, Jesus Christ, for comforting me and for providing family and friends to soothe my painful heart in times of distress. I magnify His Holy Name for giving me peace of mind and for keeping me focused during my bitter moments. His name ought to be magnified! There is no God beside Him. The prophet Isaiah reminds us of this significant fact when God inspired him to write "I *am* [Italics supplied] the LORD, and *there is* no other; *There is* no God besides Me. I will gird you, though you have not known Me, that they may know from the rising of the sun to its setting that *there is* none besides Me. I *am* the LORD, and *there is* no other; *But* Israel shall be saved by the LORD With an everlasting salvation; You shall not be ashamed or disgraced Forever and ever. For thus says the LORD, Who created the heavens, Who is God, Who formed the earth and made it, Who has established it, Who did not create it in vain, Who formed it to be inhabited: 'I *am* the LORD, and *there is* no other. Tell and bring forth *your case;* Yes, let them take counsel together. Who has declared this from ancient time? *Who* has told it from that time? *Have* not I, the LORD? And *there is* no other God besides Me, A just God and a Savior; *There is* none besides Me. Look to Me, and be saved, All you ends of the earth! For I *am* God, and *there is* no other' " (45:5, 6, 17, 18, 21, 22, NJKV). He is beyond comparison. Oh how mighty is He!

There seemed to be an ongoing struggle between my passion or will and God's plan. Although deep on the inside I knew my mission for that time was to be a mentor for the youth of this local congregation, I seemed to allow my academic pursuits to overshadow the vision and God's plan for my life. The emotional trauma marks out the journey of the true and honest individual who longs to find his/her niche in this life. It's a battle within the heart. Our world often seems rosy, pleasant, prosperous and full of great prospects. How much more could God achieve through us when we forego the human-divine fight and let His Spirit guide us on the path He has set out for us. Pain seemed to be mine major fundamental existential and emotional experience which shaped me into the individual I should have become. On reflection, I treasure the results because I realize that had I not gone through that path, I would not be able to rise to the great challenges which were to come.

What was the source of these moments of agony? Were they instigated by God? Were they brought on by God to attract my attention to His plans for my life? It is difficult to pinpoint the reasons behind these experiences, but one thing is certain. I have learnt many lessons from them and they acted as a spiritual map by directing me to God. I knocked on Heaven's door so that my Father may open the windows of Heaven and shower his many blessing on me. I challenge you that even in the midst of your darkest hour when you are ruffled by circumstances, do not give up. As we journey through life, we become agitated by personal issues, we are disconcerted and shaken by situations. But Christ, the Saviour of the world and the hope of the human race, is nearby, through the aid of the Holy Ghost, ready to soothe and comfort you. He uses human arms and shoulders to give the comfort you need. It's a resource we can tap into during our moments of agony.

Taking Time For Reflection [Jot down your thoughts]

- What was the most devastating moment in your life so far?

- How did you overcome that moment?

- If you had another chance, what would you do differently now that you have read these six chapters?

- How have your pain and wounds been made whole?

- In reflecting on what has been happening in your own life, what is it that you are (have been) uneasy about?

- In what way(s) has this chapter challenged you about your present and past life?

7
Spiritually Blind

"...If the blind lead the blind, both shall fall into the ditch" (Mt 15:14, KJV)

Some three million Americans suffer from glaucoma, a persistent eye disease that damages the optic nerve and causes blindness if left untreated. The disease usually develops without early symptoms and progresses slowly. It may occur in one or both eyes. The American National Eye Institute estimates that 120,000 Americans are blind because of glaucoma, 50 million Americans are at risk, and half the people with the disease do not know they have it. Glaucoma is the leading cause of blindness in African-Americans and the second leading cause of blindness in all Americans. Scientists are still in search of the underlying cause of glaucoma. It remains a mystery. [27]

Jesus reappeared to the disciples, just after Peter had declared boldly,

"I go a fishing" (Jn. 21:3).

The others who were with him, responded, "We also go with thee" (v.3b)

Why were they going back to their old trade at this time? Didn't they know that they were called to a higher calling? Was it unbelief in their Master? Could Peter have been unaware of Christ's plan for his life? What could have accounted for this lack of vision? Spiritual blindness!

What really motivated them to take to the sea? Could it be that they had a need for affiliation and therefore the others joined in to save their face and remain part of the in-group? We also behave like that by following others because we don't want to be left out of the inner circle. Was there a need for them to go fishing in the sea? Jesus had blessed them earlier by breathing the Holy Spirit on them. Jesus meant what He said in Luke 24:49, when He told them to remain in Jerusalem until they were endued with power from on high. It seemed to be a case of an absence of spiritual vision.

It seems evident that many Christian believers are blind spiritually with respect to God's guidance. When we fail to recognise the Hand of God in our lives, we can only conclude that we lack spiritual eyesight. While we possess the physical visual acuity, it seems to be the opposite with this spiritual sense. Interestingly, the state of blindness is prevalent in the Scriptures. It's a theological motif that signals darkness in one's life, lack of direction and the absence of spiritual discernment. Being blind spiritually highlights a case of individuals being visionless. Scripture tells that "Balak sent other princes, more numerous and more distinguished than the first. Come and put a curse on these people for me.' But Balaam answered them, 'Even if Balak gave me his palace filled with silver and gold, I could not do anything great or small to go beyond the command of the Lord my God. Now stay here tonight as the others did, and I will find out what else the Lord will tell me.' That night God came to Balaam and said, 'Since these men have come to summon you, go with them, but do only what I tell you.' Balaam got up in the morning, saddled his donkey and went with the princes of Moab. But God was very angry when he went, and the angel of the Lord stood in the road to oppose him. Balaam was riding on his donkey, and his two servants were with him. When the donkey saw the angel of the Lord standing in the road with a drawn sword in his hand, she turned off the road into a field. Balaam beat her to get her back on the road" (Num. 22:15-23, NIV). What caused Balaam to react in this way? What causes us to fight with God when we do not get our own way? Situations and events such as these require us to step back and engage in spiritual stock-taking.

The author continues to unravel the story, "Then the angel of the Lord stood in a narrow path between two vineyards, with walls on both sides. When the donkey saw the angel of the Lord, she pressed close to the wall, crushing Balaam's foot against it. So he beat her again. Then the angel of the Lord moved on ahead and stood in a narrow place where there was no room to turn, either to the right or to the left. When the donkey saw the angel of the Lord, she lay down under Balaam, and he was angry and beat her with his staff. Then the Lord opened the donkey's mouth, and she said to Balaam, 'What have I done to you to make you beat me these three times?' Balaam answered the donkey, 'You have made a fool of me! If I had a sword in my hand, I would kill you right now.' The donkey said to Balaam, 'Am I not your own donkey, which you have always ridden, to this day? Have I been in the habit of doing this to you?' 'No,' he said. Then the Lord opened Balaam's eyes, and he saw the angel of the Lord standing in the road with his sword drawn. So he bowed low and fell facedown. The angel of the Lord asked him, 'Why have you beaten your donkey these three times? I have come here to oppose you because your path is a reckless one before me. The donkey saw me and turned away from me these three times. If she had not turned away, I would certainly have killed you by now, but I would have spared her.' Balaam said to the angel of the Lord, 'I did not realize you were standing in the road to oppose me. Now if you are displeased, I will go back'" (Num. 22:24-34, NIV). Inspite of the fact that Balaam had his physical eyesight in tact, he could not discern the Angelic Being who was prepared to slaughter him for his disobedience.

Philip J. Budd alerts us to the view that "This supposed 'expert' *{Balam}* in discerning the mind and will of the gods is outperformed in spiritual insight by his donkey! His cruel treatment of the animal, in contrast to its own reasoned response, only accentuates his blindness and folly."[28] How often are we spiritually in contact with the God of Heaven? We, in this contemporary society, experience a similar fate. We lack the spiritual eyesight that would enable us to recognize the divine leading in our lives. We hardly see how God is leading us because at times our focus seems to be on the natural as opposed to spiritual issues in life. We are not always spiritually observant. That's why to have spiritual eyesight requires a high level of spiritual maturity and spirituality.

As I reflect on my past experiences, something occurred to me one day while I was teaching a Year 4 class. I was using a story by Browne & Campbell (1984) entitled "Brer Annancy and the Alligator Eggs" to prepare the students for the day's academic work. The two fish characters in the story had impairments: hearing and communication disorder. The two fish were communicating with each other, but as the authors depicted the story, neither of the fish understood the other. While one of the fish could speak well, the other could not understand what was being said. It suddenly appeared to me as I was reading the story that I could have an impairment: a spiritual eye problem. This thought struck me like dynamite, shook my inner being to the core, and caused me to engage in some stock-taking. What could have brought on this myopia? I began to examine my spiritual life. What was I doing wrong?

Where am I with God? As I continue to search my inner being, I realised that I was spiritually blind.

I was travelling headlong engaging in my academic pursuits and was saying simultaneously to myself that I knew the real purpose for my being in the UK. Although I was fully involved in church activities, I was caught up like the other students with completing assignments. The C+ for my first set of assignments should have told me that something was not right. I had prayed and fasted over these assignments, and I couldn't understand why I was given 57% and 58% which were a few marks short of grade Bs (60%), the required grade. I endeavoured to do much better on the other two assignments since the time for my doctoral upgrading was near. On reflection, I realised that there was blindness and worst yet, short-sightedness, because I failed to see the bigger picture. Often times we don't see the macro picture that God is displaying before us. We become engrossed in the events of the moment and although there are signals that tell us something is not right, our dark blindness prohibits us from envisioning what God is trying to show us.

When we examine the Elisha's experience with Yahweh, we encounter the biblical story informing us that "The king of Aram was at war with Israel. After conferring with his officers, he said, 'will set up my camp in such and such a place.' The man of God sent word to the king of Israel: 'Beware of passing that place, because the Arameans are going down there.' So the king of Israel checked on the place indicated by the man of God. Time and again Elisha warned the king, so that he was on his guard in such places. This enraged the king of Aram. He summoned his officers and demanded of them, 'Will you not tell me which of us is on the side of the king of Israel?' 'None of us, my lord the king,' said one of his officers, 'but

Elisha, the prophet who is in Israel, tells the king of Israel the very words you speak in your bedroom.' 'Go, find out where he is,' the king ordered, 'so I can send men and capture him.' They went by night and surrounded the city. When the servant of the man of God got up and went out early the next morning, an army with horses and chariots had surrounded the city. 'Oh, my lord, what shall we do?' the servant asked. 'Don't be afraid,' the prophet answered. 'Those who are with us are more than those who are with them.' And Elisha prayed, 'O Lord, open his eyes so he may see.' Then the Lord opened the servant's eyes, and he looked and saw the hills full of horses and chariots of fire all around Elisha" (2 Kgs 6:8-17, NIV). The inept spiritual condition of the prophet's servant prevented him from seeing the innumerable host of mighty Angelic Beings who surrounded the area. Can you imagine the fear that must have gripped Elisha's servant? What emotion grips us as our journey become dark and we grope in obscurity trying to achieve the unreachable?

John, the writer of the Fourth Gospel, recounts a further example of blindness in the Scripture:"Now as *Jesus* passed by, He saw a man who was blind from birth. And His disciples asked Him, saying, 'Rabbi, who sinned, this man or his parents, that he was born blind?' Jesus answered, 'Neither this man nor his parents sinned, but that the works of God should be revealed in him. I must work the works of Him who sent Me while it is day; *the night* is coming when no one can work. As long as I am in the world, I am the light of the world'. When He had said these things, He spat on the ground and made clay with the saliva; and He anointed the eyes of the blind man with the clay. And He said to him, 'Go, wash in the pool of Siloam' (which is translated, Sent). So he went and washed, and came back seeing. Therefore the neighbors and those who previously had seen that he was blind said, 'Is not this he who sat and begged?'"(9:1-8, NJKV). Although we are uncertain as to how many blind individuals Jesus healed, we see in this episode that He took the initiative to restore the man's sight. The importance of sight is demonstrated through the healing of two other blind men by Jesus (Mk 8:22-25; 10:46-52). We live in a society which places a high value on physical eyesight. We also need to demonstrate the importance of having spiritual eyesight. A lack of it can be costly.

The disciples' spiritual blindness kept them from focussing on God's purpose for their lives, to the extent that they wasted their time and energy at sea. Why? "That night they caught nothing" (Jn 21.3, NIV). Is it a wonder when we are spiritually blind that we lose track of our goal and aim? Even when we may be busy with church activities and humanitarian efforts, we still come up empty-handed. Our busy schedule is no substitute for the spirituality that is needed to propel each of us onto being where God wants us to be. But such a situation echoes the disciples' plight as well as mine. It is affirmed by the insightful words: "Where there is no vision, the people perish" (Prov. 29:18).

Three types of spiritual sights: foresight, insight, and hindsight are vital in accomplishing God's purpose for us. The God of Heaven gives us wisdom to look ahead with a vision or a plan which is Christ-centred and realistic. But they will certainly be achieved. The question we must ask ourselves is: Do I have a vision? What does the Lord want to accomplish through me in the near future? I dare say that the twenty-first century in which we live is not the era in which we should be contented with nothing. It's not the time to be led by others or to allow other people to achieve and we applaud their efforts. We need to pray for a spiritual vision, for foresight. Looking ahead with God's eyes!

One way of being helped, particularly in times of social deprivation, social upheaval, and societal difficulties, is through the Scriptures. Moreover, if we want to gain the needed assistance from this resource, we need to gain insight from the Word. Trying circumstances require that we receive in-depth spiritual messages from the Scriptures so that they may hold us up, strengthen our faith, and re-assure us that the Master is still working on our behalf. Additionally, we need to be capable of sharing the message we have found with friends, family and foes alike. To do otherwise is to lose the opportunity to help a desperate individual who doesn't know what to do with his/her life.

The episode in St. John 21 suggests that Peter was operating on hindsight to the point that he failed to realise that Jesus was standing on the sea-shore with his keen eyes upon them. The writer of John's Gospel recalls that "Thomas, one of the twelve, called Didymus, was not with them when Jesus came. The other disciples therefore said unto him, We have seen the Lord. But he said unto them, Except I shall see in his hands the print of the nails, and put my finger into the print of the nails, and thrust my hand into his side, I will not believe. And after eight days again his disciples were within, and Thomas with them: then came Jesus, the doors being shut, and stood in the midst, and said, Peace be unto you. Then saith he to Thomas, Reach hither thy finger, and behold my hands; and reach hither thy hand, and thrust it into my side: and be not faithless, but believing. And Thomas answered and said unto him, My Lord and my God. Jesus saith unto him, Thomas, because thou hast seen me, thou hast believed: blessed are they that have not seen, and yet have believed. And many other signs truly did Jesus in the presence of his disciples, which are not written in this book: But these are written, that ye might believe that Jesus is the Christ, the Son of God; and that believing ye might have life through his name (Jn 20:23-31). None of the events in this episode jolted the disciples' mind that Jesus was serious when he told them to wait until the Holy Ghost empowered them. It took another miraculous event before they shouted, "It is the Lord" (Jn 21:7).

Interestingly, when we are confronted by divine interventions, we attempt to ignore them by using psychological defences, allowing memory lapses and putting up psychological barriers so as not to recognise the voice which is calling out to us. Although all of the answers to my prayers for funding came back with an emphatic 'no', I was too determined that no matter what, I was going through with this degree. I still held the philosophy that as a Christian, I should do all that is in my power with honesty and the Lord will do his part. I never for one moment considered that the Lord was saying a definite 'no' to my studies. I seemed to have lost focus of my principal reason for being in the United Kingdom and was more concerned with the secondary focus (my studies). I seemed to have lost focus of my principal purpose by veering off course. Have you gone off track? Have you forgotten your purpose in life? Will you wait for severe upheavals to awaken you? You do not have to be spiritually blind!

Taking Time For Reflection [Jot down your thoughts]

- Do you believe that what you are doing is not what you should be actually doing?

- Have there been signs that have been alerting you to this, but you have continued to ignore them?

- What would you need to help you find your true place in life so that you may fulfil your true purpose?

8
The Call

"He invites us to give ourselves to Him, that He may work His will in us...In giving ourselves to God, we must necessarily give up all that would separate us from Him" (White, *Steps to Christ*, 2000: 29)

Some of the ordinary people in Jesus' time were "public failures like Simon Peter and men of irascible temperament like the two sons of Zebedee."[29] They seemed contented with their social position in life: that of being fishermen. These men appeared conscientious and industrious workers. Some were mending their nets and others were by the seaside strategically hurling their nets into the sea when Jesus caught sight of them (Mk. 1.18-20). Others such as Matthew and Luke, although from the upper echelons of society, also appeared to be satisfied with their earthly position.

Jesus' appearance by the Galilean Sea sparked a new beginning for a group of men who never dreamed of such a turn of events in their lives. Mark, the Second Evangelist in the New Testament, illustrates how Jesus positioned himself for taking the initiative in extending His invitation: "Now as he [Jesus] walked by the Sea of Galilee, he saw Simon and Andrew his brother casting a net into the sea: for they were fishers" (Mk 1:16). The Master's invitation, "come ye after me and I will make you to become fishers of men" (Mk.1.17) was unexpected and surprising. Many thoughts probably rushed through their heads. Did they ever think of working with Jesus or even becoming Christians? What prompted them to accept this divine call? Did he attract them with their own profession, by giving them a paradigm shift? Did he help them to see their purpose in this life from a new perspective? The invitation that Jesus extended to these fishermen appeared to be an abrupt one. There was no prior warning, no opportunity for farewell speeches, and no opportunity to settle debts. Evans informs us that "Mark may have wished to impress upon his readers the authority of Jesus. When He extends a summons, people jump. Little or no ceremony is required."[30] Jesus' authority and influence were so effective that "straightway they forsook their nets, and followed him" (Mk. 1:17). The extent of this powerful influence prevailed strongly. John and his brother, James "left their father Zebedee in the ship with the hired servants, and went after him" (Mk. 1:20). Whatever were their reasons, they responded to the call, which became the means by which their lives were transformed. Discerningly, Jesus used the disciples' trade to attract them to Him. He met them in their sphere of life and in the place where they were kings: in the sea. Similarly, God often comes to us where we are most comfortable: in our office, on our farm or in the trenches and extends His invitation to us. Our response determines the outcome in our lives.

In turning to my past situation, I recall vividly my years as a lay preacher, when there were numerous opportunities for me to preach in many congregations. It is a work that thrills me and brings great joy and satisfaction. Additionally, I have been involved in many evangelistic events such as bible studies and evangelistic campaigns. Through these events, by being a member of pastoral teams and in leadership positions, I have been able to provide pastoral care to various individuals. At the end of many church services, both in the Caribbean and in the UK, as the members exit the church, some of those who are well acquainted with me would ask, "Why don't you go into pastoral ministry?"

I would often respond by saying, "Let the Lord lead! I cannot move untimely." At other times I would respond with the words, "That's not my calling."

What were they saying? Did they see or know something that I did not know? Could these faithful believers perceive beyond the present time and recognise the *Hand of God* on my life? Why was the issue of pastoral ministry constantly drawn to my attention? It is possible that the writing was on the wall, but, because I was spiritually blind, I could not see it. It could also be that, like the boy, Samuel in the temple serving Eli, the Israelite priest, I had "not yet know the Lord" (1 Sam.3.7). God often uses human influence to guide us on the path that He has mapped out for us. It's his providential nature emerging to attract our attention. But all too often we seldom heed to this type of guidance. The providential working of God emerges, only for us, who lack the spiritual foresight to squander our chances.

Frankly speaking, I never dreamed of or desired to engage in full-time pastoral ministry. There were many aspirations: to be a psychiatric nurse, teacher or university lecturer, but I never dreamt of being a pastor. I did not envisage myself becoming a pastor, perhaps because I could not see beyond my secular career of being a teacher and my dream to be an educational psychologist. Deep within the recesses of my heart I knew that the Lord wanted me to be the mentor to the group of young people with whom I worshipped in the UK. I have been involved in Christian youth work for more than half of my life as a Christian. So getting involved in this type of activity was not unusual. However, I was never aware of any promptings or hints of being trained for pastoral ministry. But is this really the case? Admittedly, I checked the website of the Adventist training college in the UK on two occasions. I am not sure what prompted this curiosity, but it was short-lived.

What attracted my attention to the divine call? How did I know that pastoral ministry was God's plan for me? I had already planned to return to my Caribbean home, with the intention of pursuing doctoral studies from there. I felt that I had accomplished the mission that God had placed on my heart. Having that sense of satisfaction and achievement, I wasn't prepared to stay around any longer. My academic success up to this point propelled me to pursue doctoral studies. Besides, I was not interested in returning to the classroom at the primary school level. Everything was in place: I had bought the airline ticket and was packing my clothes and books. I had also informed my family that I was returning home.

When I broke the news of me taking the next flight back home, my wife asked in a very concerned manner,

"Are you sure you want to come back now?"

"I am very sure. I did what I was supposed to do," I responded.

"But your studies haven't finished," she pressed further.

"I must leave," I added persistently.

"If that's what you say. Josiah will be glad to see and have you back," my wife concluded.

I waited patiently, but anxiously and eagerly for my departure date. As the end of the chilly autumn was approaching, my plans were intercepted in a marked and visible way. Just when I thought that I was about to launch out and achieve my dream by continuing Ph D studies, the flood-gates opened once more.

It was in the early hours of the last Monday, October 2001, during my devotions that I was praying earnestly that the Lord would direct me. I was on my knees in my upstairs flat. My room was very quiet, seeing that it was early in the morning. The wind on the outside was whistling profusely as it beat against the double-glaze window. The condensed ice water trickled down the window pane. I wanted something more than just the norm of life or the hum-drum. I was tired with the same old usual things of life. I was desperate to move beyond the spiritual surface.

"Lord, there has to be something more that you have in store for me," I pleaded that dark morning.

I was yearning for something more. My spiritual journey up to this point had taken on a new level and I refused to be contented with where I was at that time. As I reached out in prayer, calling out to the God of Heaven, a voice spoke audibly, distinctly and forcibly, "Ministry." Immediately, *I felt the Hand of God* over my head and I sensed that His presence was over me so powerfully, that I wept uncontrollably. The tears rushed down my slender cheeks. My heart was very heavy. This experience was unimaginable and totally unexpected. It felt as if God was sitting on the periphery of my life just waiting for me to open my heart honestly to Him so that He could take over. It was difficult for me to move. So my only resolve there and then was to weep, stay on my knees, and listen more intently. It was a bitter moment. That famous hymn penned by Ralph Carmichael (1958) that brought tears to my eyes in early 2000 came back, "The Savior is waiting to enter your heart, why don't you let him come in." I did not feel like moving, worst yet I could not move. My physical frame was numb. A feeling of helplessness came over me. My running was over. The inner fight had ended. I yielded to the divine call.

By this time it was probably 7 a.m. because the cellular phone rang. I picked it up and answered through my tears. It was one of my pastors. During that week, we were prayer partners based on a programme that he had initiated during prayer meeting. Was this coincidental or divinely designed? I continued to cry bitterly. The voice asked, "Are you ok?"

"No!" I said in all honesty.

Indeed, I was not and could not be ok, seeing that my life and all of my plans had just taken a one hundred and eighty degrees turn. My world had just turned upside down. I sensed that I had lost control of my life. I no longer could decide what I wanted to do with my life. The Hand of God was upon me. The atmosphere was awesome. There was a mixture of inner feelings: sadness, grief, anger, and joy. I could not believe it.

Soon after, Pastor Trimble inquired about the reason for my tears and I related the entire story to him.

"The Lord has just spoken to me," I shared, still crying out.

"Oh, Victor!" he sighed.

"How did it happen?" he queried.

"I was here reaching out in prayer and I heard a voice saying 'Ministry' and the same time I felt this hand over my head," I replied tearfully.

"It's not the best of times for you?" he said cautiously.

"I never ever thought of going into fulltime pastoral ministry. This is not what I wanted. It's very painful," I responded.

The tears were still dripping from my cloudy eyes. The more I tried to hold them back, the more they flowed. The pain gripped me. My wounds were fully opened. The incision was vastly deep.

"That was similar to my call to ministry," he informed me.

I could well imagine how he felt.

Immediately after the conversation, he prayed with me, counselled me and encouraged me. It is times like these, that human ears and shoulders are a source of strength. They become the cushion to soothe the pain. The human presence is a great treasure. Eventually, I came to myself, still shaken, but totally pensive. *What steps should I take? What should I do now?* I pondered in my mind. It was time for action.

Later, I informed my supervisor in the department where I was a student that I was quitting the programme.

"What made you come to this decision," he asked.

"I feel God is calling me to full-time church work," I responded.

"That's a sudden jump," he added.

"Don't you want to continue the programme first," he questioned.

"I just can't. I feel I must go now," I reiterated.

"Well best of luck. Have you written the department? You will need to." He informed me.

"I will," I said.

No amount of prompting would have changed my mind. I was fully convinced that Jehovah-Rohi, the Lord my Shepherd, was guiding me. There was going to be no turning back.

I returned all the books to the library and began channelling my mind in a new direction. I checked the website of the Adventist training College in Britain for information, downloaded the necessary documents and completed them. In the meantime, I approached a number of individuals to obtain references, secured all the other necessary documents and prepared for theological studies.

The events of that week sparked a new beginning for me. I was very reflective. I was willing to allow the Lord to direct me in every area. I spoke with Pastor Slater, the senior pastor and he came over to visit me.

"How are you doing?" he asked.

"I am not sure. I believe that God is calling me to full-time pastoral ministry," I replied rather quietly.

"Umm! How did that happen?" he inquired further.

"I was praying and I heard a voice saying 'Ministry'. I know this is the Lord speaking because this is not what I had planned to do," I replied.

"When did it happen?" he asked.

Last Monday, early in the morning," I replied.

How do you feel about it?" he inquired.

"I believe that it is the Lord, because I never had this in mind," I responded.

"Does your family know?" he probed.

"No. I haven't told them as yet," I added.

"It is important that your family joins you. If they are not coming with you, it makes no sense becoming involved in fulltime ministry. It's better that you go home and tell them face to face," he counselled.

"OK," I replied.

After we spoke, he prayed for me. It was divine thunder that riveted through my world, thus causing many questions to fill my mind. Why did the Lord take so long to lead me into pastoral ministry? Why did he have to take me to the UK to bring me face to face with his will for my life? Did he impress on my mind to take up full-time pastoral work prior to this time? Why did he have to allow me to go through such trials to bring me to this point? When I reflect on this experience, I am willing to agree with Partow's admission that "...he can use the most unlikely vessels to accomplish his purposes- yes, even the greatest purpose in the history of human civilization."[31]

My theophany (encounter with God) marked the end of the tensions that I had experienced during this two years. It had implications for my life hereafter. It was this painful experience that brought the final end to the tension between the Ministry of Education and myself, between God and me over my doctoral studies, and, more powerfully, between the university and myself. It was the guiding event that allowed me to understand the importance of surrendering. With my emotional wounds so fresh, tears constantly flowing down my cheeks, my back against a wall, nowhere to turn and no human help possible, I had to give in.

I continue to bear the scars in my mind. They are truly deep and lengthy. Each time I am impressed to share this testimony, I weep bitterly. I remember the day as if it were yesterday. It seems to be my 'thorn in the flesh' to keep me focus on the fact that God has called me so that He may accomplish His purpose through me. The willingness to accept our new role in life must be inward and as Partow concluded, "…it doesn't matter where you've been. It doesn't matter what mistakes you've made. If you will turn your heart to God, you can become a vessel God can use."[32]

Turning to the disciples' response to Jesus' call, I believe that it was one of immediacy, to the extent that they were unconcerned about issues such as the safety of their boats, dispensing with the vessels and such the like. Some folks may surmise that their response was based on evidence of God's ability to provide and protect them. However, from their new encounter with their Master, they had a priority shift. Within their minds they were determined to obey, follow his leading and respond to the call. They were on the brink of travelling on a road that would eventually lead them to become the men who "turned the world upside down" (Acts 17.6).

Have you been clutching on to a career because it provides peace of mind or because you are emotionally comfortable? Are you holding on to a dream that is rapidly sliding out of your grasp and you have no control of the slide? Is the field of study you are pursuing providing you with a rosy future? Do you perceive that you are being led in a particular direction for which you had never planned? Maybe your life is helter-skelter and has no resting place. It is worth pondering on such questions since it is highly probable that you can be confronted with some of them as you journey through this life searching for a purpose in life.

__Taking Time For Reflection__ [Jot down your thoughts]

- Has there been an inner urge to make some changes in your life?

- What is in your life at the present moment that is hindering you from making those changes?

- How helpful would human presence be in aiding you at this time?

- Maybe you have been challenged greatly by this chapter. How willing are you to take up that challenge?

- What (who) might hinder you from making the changes you want to make

9
Power in the Ministry of Presence

"Peace to you from God our Father ,...the Father of compassion and the God of all comfort, who comforts us in all our troubles, so that we can comfort those in any trouble with the comfort we ourselves have received..."(2 Cor. 1:2-4, NIV)

You were in my thoughts today. I have been praying for you son. Hi, Vic, I just came over to see how you are doing.' Do these words sound familiar? Maybe they do. These are the type of sentiments people express as a means of demonstrating their concern for us. So what's so exciting about all of this? Well, this is what helps us battle our moments of loneliness, seclusion and exclusion. When we are down and out, going through our 'valleys of death', down in the dumps, struggling in the mirth, and feel that we are alone, that is when we need to hear such words. I believe this type of activity is powerful, particularly in the lives of those who are experiencing pain and are wounded from some shattering experience or who are at a lost as to what to do with their lives. It's the ministry of presence that contributes to our healing and to us finding meaning in our lives.

A major event of my social life during the two years I spent in this Yorkshire city was attending youth club ever Saturday night, particularly in the winter months. I met some of the senior and young members of the congregation where I worshipped, thereby becoming more acquainted with other individuals. The nights were spent playing games such as dominoes and dodge ball, letting of the steam from a hard week's work or studies, eating delicious food and chatting with each other. Dodge ball was the most exciting for us. It evoked loud laughter and screeching shouts. It was competitive. Our head deacon would make some delicious crisp, brown 'festivals' along with vegetarian burgers. The festivals, an elongated fried bun, were the desire of every club member. Most times some of the young people attended club just to grab the scarce delicacy. For me, it was a night out in an appropriate environment and being engaged in wholesome activities. I was away from my lonely university flat where I had the options of sleeping, watching television, or studying. But this was not of interest to me on Saturday nights when I simply wanted to socialise. I was experiencing what Collins classified as "transient-situational loneliness...because of my move to college [*university*]...."[33] I believe I was going through a patch of loneliness because I hadn't linked up with friends as yet. The feeling of sadness was the major symptom that I was displaying. As time went on and I made contact with other friends, this short-lived loneliness turned to solitude. Psychologist Gary Collins makes the distinction between loneliness and solitude where "...solitude is a voluntary withdrawal from other people...solitude can be started and terminated at will....solitude can be refreshing, rejuvenating and enjoyable."[34] It may be a true case generally, but for me it was profoundly difficult to be confined to my room or to the library. But, as time rushed by, my situation changed where a family found me and drew me under their loving wings.

My flat mates went pub-crawling on Friday nights and Saturday nights, but this was not in my mind. There was no way I would engage in such an activity. It simply was not in my repertoire. This was the reason I looked forward to youth club because it saved me from an isolated world even though I was among thousands of students: national, regional and international. Such isolation loudly echoes Gary Collins' perception that "loneliness is the painful awareness that we lack close and meaningful contact with others. It involves a feeling of inner emptiness, isolation and intense longing. Even when they are surrounded by others, lonely people often feel left out…." [35] The need to belong was there and I had to find a way of meeting such a need. It's a higher order psychological need which is satisfied by developing interpersonal relationships with friends, family members or a group. Being away from my biological family meant that the most appropriate way for this need to be met was to be associated with people of like mind and who had similar values to mine. We must recognise that this need arises from the mega need, which is the need for affiliation. Our anthropological make-up calls for social connections where we seek to develop and maintain relationships with others. Being deprived of this type of socialisation leads us to develop feelings of rejection and loneliness.

When there was no youth club, house socials replaced it. This was even more fun. We would organise transportation based on those who owned cars and drive to different members' homes where we would play various games, many of which I did not have a clue about. Because of the limited cars, on a few occasions, we had to bundle into the available cars. Some of the games stretched my imagination and thinking. Many times I would monitor the games leader's action intently by listening to his words, watching his hands, eyes, and listening to his cunning clues. Ironically, many of these games do not have names. I would strain my ears and widen my eyes, all in an effort to get the gist of the game. And yet many times the games still eluded me. But as I observed, I caught on quickly and I was soon out of my misery.

"Let me try this one," I would anxiously blurt out as I learnt the games.

"Let's see if Vic got it as yet," one of the leaders would say.

I would lead out in the particular game and after giving the correct response, one of the young people who knew the games would say rather reluctantly,

"He got it."

We wanted other people to learn the games, but we also wanted to keep them as a secret. With a few people being able to spot the clue, this adds excitement, suspense and delight to the games. These socials activities were wonderful. It was a time of bonding with each other as we spent many hours together into the early part of many Sunday mornings. It was at these events that I became more acquainted with names, family connections and who were the leaders in the congregation. These events helped give me inner strength to face the challenges of the week, both with my studies and in the classroom as I worked doing supply teaching.

Apart from the eating and playing of games, there were times when individuals would have one-to-one chats with me about my field of studies and how the assignments were progressing. By being invited out to concerts and games night, it demonstrated to me that people cared for me and were interested in my welfare. I felt involved and this helped me to regain my sense of belonging. They wanted to ensure that I was not out of my depths. It's through such sessions that you get a grip of those who you can trust and with whom you can share your inner thoughts and feeling. By having these kinds of individuals around, we discover those we can open up to and share the issues that are pressing on us forcibly.

Occasions like these were more about connecting and socialising than going to events. There are times, particularly in the summer months that I did not attend some of the trips or events that the other young people were attending. But, beyond this, as young people we always had some major event to attend whether it was a concert at another church, a student day programme or simply taking a walk in the nearby tropical world park. Many Sunday mornings were spent in one of the nearby local parks having morning devotions in the glistening sunshine. Interestingly, the summer was the time to get out as a group and it gave me the opportunity to meet other people, become acquainted with other British places and see how worship is conducted by other people. It gave me a chance to see that the type of worship or the environment at my local home church was not the only way that church life was conducted here. I enjoyed going places with my friends, the famous twelve.

Pondering for a while on Gal. 6:2, which reads: "Carry each other's burdens, and in this way you will fulfil the law of Christ" made me thought about its meaning for a while. I reflected on how it fitted into my experience. As I applied it to my life, I recognised that the word 'carry' had a far-reaching meaning in that it denotes the idea of supporting and sustaining each other. Of all the variant meanings, this one fits well. We see how critical it is to be there for others. Our mere presence, the striking up of a conversation or enquiring about each other's welfare, are all part of what I describe as the ministry of presence. We are there with the individual, silent at times, but also verbally interacting with them. We are actively engaged, helping them to find their 'footing'. By doing this, we are helping them, through the aid of the Holy Spirit, to find their way.

One of the greatest and most powerful aspects of the ministry of presence is to have human hands to lift you up when you are going under. We become Christ in the flesh to those around us and demonstrate what Christ would have done had he been there with us physically. This is where the power of prayer is played out in each other's lives so dramatically. It's a spiritual resource that becomes effective in the lives of individuals, particularly when we intercede aggressively for that person. Through prayer, those hands become the hands of God. Just as Jesus did to Simon Peter who was about to sink, we can rescue each other from drowning in their ocean of misery, debt, pressure, despair and depression. What would have happen had you not responded to that call that you received from that friend? Where would that individual be now had you not given him/her the dire help that was needed at the time?

Human ears and shoulders are also powerful elements in the ministry of presence that become cushions for helpless individuals. Bearing each other's burdens is more than just taking on the issue for or with the individual. It's also about being a listening ear to their concerns in a confidential manner. It's about allowing them to see that you can be trusted and that confidentiality is not breached. It's about knowing that someone is there on whom we can lean, who will hold us up when we are weak and frail from the wounds we bear or from the frustration that we are going through at the moment.

The ministry of presence is in contrast to Cain's cowardly and pessimistic response "I don't know...Am I my brother's keeper?" (Gen. 4:9, NIV). His aggressive and high-tempered response to the God of Heaven epitomises a familiar behaviour in us as human beings to focus on self and forget the hurting and the marginalised people around. His response highlights that perennial mortal response where we sideline those on the periphery and those who don't seem to have much to offer. It's a case of us versus them. It is somewhat startling that Cain did not know or have a present awareness of his brother's whereabouts. We use psychological mechanisms such as rationalisation and projection to avoid showing interest in those with whom we are least concerned. This Cain-Abel affair stirs up a stark reality where we often don't know the whereabouts of each other, particularly those we are not close to, we tend not to check for each other and at times we couldn't be bothered to inquire.

The writer of Genesis, the first pentateuchal book, tells us that "Cain said to his brother Abel, 'Let's go out to the field.' And while they were in the field, Cain attacked his brother Abel and killed him. Then the Lord said to Cain, 'Where is your brother Abel?' 'I do not know,' he replied. 'Am I my brother's keeper?' The Lord said, 'What have you done? Listen! Your brother's blood cries out to me from the ground. Now you are under a curse and driven from the ground, which opened its mouth to receive your brother's blood from your hand'" (Gen. 4:8-11, NIV). Importantly, the word *brother* is a significant theological motif in this episode in that with the repetitious occurrence of such a term, we cannot shy away from the close connection and relations that are portrayed through the use of this word *brother*. What was Cain saying to Jehovah? Was he saying that there was no relationship between his *brother*, Abel and himself? Was he saying that he had severed all connections and ties with Abel? What could we be saying when we fail to connect with each other? The initial relationship that Cain, the first-born, had with his *brother* prior to bringing their respective offerings to the God of Heaven seemed to have dictated the course of events after the rejection of his {Cain's} offering. So what kind of relationship was it? Was it closely knitted, fragile, loose, marginal, or stormy? The familial ties should have been enough to awaken Cain, to his individual responsibility, but instead, he denied his part and role in being his *brother's* keeper. It was the least of his worries at that time. No wonder he could have easily got rid of Abel! Everyone who talks with us is not with us! So it is vital that relationships are maintained genuinely through prayer and fellowship. By extension, we must be willing to step up to the challenge of being there for others around us. It is important that we indicate to others that they also matter because God cares for them too. The ministry of presence is vital to each other's socialisation process. It can contribute to us finding God's plan for us because it is through others that he speaks at times to make us aware of his plan for our life.

Taking Time for Reflection {Jot down your thoughts}

- What has your experience been like up to this point?

- What has been your greatest challenge in socialising with others?

- Think about any barriers that exist in your local congregation or small group. How can you assist in breaking the barrier to encourage a ministry of presence?

- Re-read Gal. 6:2 and Gen. 4:9. To what extent do each of these verses refer to you?

- Are you a hindrance to or a helper in developing a ministry of presence in your sphere of influence (among the circle of people with whom you function)?

10
Spilling the News

"In his heart a man plans his course, but the Lord determines his steps"
(Prov. 16: 9, NIV)

It was approaching winter in December 2001, when I would have to face the cold weather for the last time in this Yorkshire city and also share the devastating news. Meanwhile, there were other outstanding matters that had to be attended to immediately. As a tenant, I was legally bonded to give my landlord a month's notice of my intentions to vacate my flat. Unfortunately, the nerve-racking experiences of the summer contributed to me being unable to pay my rent for six months. Two things seemed to work in my favour: I was indebted to my local home church and I kept in contact with them by paying small portions of the rent because I could not afford anymore at the time.

I typed the letter and submitted it to the church board, informing them of my plan to leave the flat, alerted them that I was aware of my huge debt and of my intentions to repay all of it prior to my departure. I submitted the letter prior to the start of the Sabbath (Saturday) church service and by evening the head deacon came to me with the wonderful news that the church board had cleared me of all debts. Again, I saw the mighty *Hand of God* working out his will in my life as I continued to submit to his call. Moreover, he also told me that if I paid any money as of that day, it would be returned to me. I truly thank the leadership of this local congregation for their kindness, support, and thoughtfulness that they showered on me.

How should I break the news to a family that supported me through my rough journey? How do I fill the vacuum that will be created through my departure? How do I make a group of young people that I had grown to love and work with understand that I have to leave? I felt as if a part of me had been ripped away, but, on reflection, I had no choice. It had to be done. I had the painful task of relating to my adopted family the turn of events in my life and what was going to be my next step. How do I break the news that I am giving up a doctoral programme in educational psychology to pursue pastoral ministry? Will I be jeered, scoffed at or bombarded with negative comments?

I believe it was the most shattering piece of news I had to share because it brought a calm, a 'hush', and quietness to the room as I spoke. I was asked: "What brought about this change? Are you sure this is what you want?"

After explaining the dynamics that brought about the call, my adopted family counselled me to let the Lord lead. They also encouraged me to put him first in everything, reminding me that it will all work out.

I had developed close relationships with many church members. As I shared the news, some were in disbelief, some were moved, others were elated that the Lord was leading me in this direction, and a few stood in awe and surprise. The elated ones expressed their willingness to see God continual leadership in my life. They encouraged me and praised God for moving so mightily. Others chipped in with the response,

"I know the Lord will come through for you. Everything will work out. We will be praying for you."

For me to leave this group of close friends was heart-wrenching, knowing that we had developed a very close relationship during our two years together.

There were a few folks who stood shocked and disappointed. They urged me to stay on the doctoral programme, adding that it would open doors wider in pastoral ministry and that I would be more recognised. It was difficult trying to convince them, but my mind was made up and I held on firmly to my decision as I vowed inwardly to follow God's directives. With my spiritual wounds fresh, I was under immense pressure and felt powerless to push off the psychological battle that was raging around me. Nevertheless, there was inner bold that helped me to face the attacks and barrage of comments.

It was time to return to the Caribbean to see Maria and Josiah again and to lay God's plan for my life at their feet. The last Sabbath I spent in the UK was heart-wrenching. I broke down in tears. It felt as if I was leaving my children unattended. *How would they survive spiritually? Would they pick up from where I left off? Will they be inspired and become zealous w*ere the thoughts that flooded and bombarded my mind. Some of the young people accompanied me to the train station. We hugged, shared our good-byes and wished each other God's guidance. We endeavoured to meet each other again. The unknown was before me. I was not certain whether I would ever meet them in this earthly life again. As I embarked the GNER Express train to London, my heart pained. The emotions were ambivalent. I was sad to be leaving them, but elated on knowing that I will see my wife and son again. I was torn in two. I had to cut the cord that bound us so close. I had to loose them and let the God that called me be the one to guide them.

Having reached my sunny Caribbean beautiful island home, I settled in and gained my footing. I spent time with everyone. We talked about the flight, about the youth and my adopted family. My son was almost touching the sky because I was back home forever. My wife's throbbing heart was settled.

"Daddy, what have you brought for me?" Josiah asked as he hurriedly zipped open suitcase number one.

"Wait! Take it easy. You will get what is for you," I cautioned him.

"Boy your father isn't going anywhere. Just wait," Maria warned.

My son was too elated to wait around. I took out the sweets, a few shirts and some shoes. His eyes lighted up like a play park covered with decoration lights on a Christmas morning. He ripped open the wrapping to taste the British sweets.

As night came on, there was the urge to spill the news.

When should I tell her? I thought to myself.

How would she take it? What would she think?

I had planned to wait for three weeks, but I just could not wait for such a long time. Around seven in the night of the same day that I arrived back home, I spoke softly and slowly saying,

"I have some news to share with you, but not now."

"What is it?" she asked.

"I don't think that you are ready for this yet," I replied.

"How do you know?" She responded. "Just tell me!"

"The Lord has impressed on my heart to study for the ministry."

She replied by saying, "I was telling you so for a long time, but you didn't think so. You said that it was not your calling."

"Is that true? I don't remember," I replied.

Unbelievable! All my fears of her disapproval had vanished. Prayers were answered. The Lord had placed this in her heart long ago. Her positive response and affirmation paved the way for us to plan mutually for this new mission.

As I shared this news with many of my friends in my Caribbean home, some displayed facial expressions that revealed unbelief. Others hugged me, shook hands, raised their heads to the heavens, and still others laughed with joy. They wished me God's blessings and expressed the view that I would succeed through God's grace and guidance. One of them was notably disappointed and horrified, by saying,

"Are you going to give up all of that to preach?"

"Jesus gave up his life for me, so why can't I give up a doctorate for his work," I replied.

"Well, true. I wish you all the best," she finally remarked.

There were a few others who did not accept my shift, perhaps because it seemed unjustified and confusing to them. The ambivalent responses from acquaintances and friends indicated to me that I had to hold onto my decision so that confusion and doubt would not reign. It seems possible that many people do not see the bigger picture. They operate from a narrow worldview and fail to widen their scope, hence to shift from such a high academic level to become a preacher of the Gospel seems outrageous. But our personality must be of such that when we are determined, nothing should move us from our decision. In psychological terms, such persons tend to be phlegmatic, of the decisive type and be unchanging in matters that have been settled.[36] How do you push off suggestions that you know are contrary to your deep inner being? How do you respond to individuals who want to turn you away from the decision you have made about a change in your personal life?

While we may be caught in a struggle trying to juggle other people's viewpoints, we need to remember that there are always consequences which follow our actions or decisions. What is painful is that we are often left 'high and dry' to bear the consequences ourselves.

The multiplicity of reactions to this news did not shake me because I knew that the Lord was leading me, His hands were moving visibly in my life, and with His courage and strength, I was determined to follow His command. It is never easy breaking this type of news because of the nature of the new mission. News of this kind is hard to swallow and it stirs different attitudes in people. Individuals tend to be ambivalent about spiritual matters and divine guidance. In spite of the mixed views, expressions, and thoughts, I was confident that God would see me through the new phase of my journey.

The task of breaking the news of this kind tests our resolution. It's the time of our life that determines how we respond to suggestions from those who are thoughtful, insightful and adventurous. We find ourselves battling against the opposition from the inconsiderate and those who lack vision. The news we despatch can be shocking to other people's minds, especially when it's least expected. In 1 Samuel we encounter a catastrophe which resulted in the receipt of bad news: "That same day a Benjamite ran from the battle line and went to Shiloh, his clothes torn and dust on his head. When he arrived, there was Eli sitting on his chair by the side of the road, watching, because his heart feared for the ark of God. When the man entered the town and told what had happened, the whole town sent up a cry. Eli heard the outcry and asked, 'What is the meaning of this uproar?' The man hurried over to Eli, who was ninety-eight years old and whose eyes were set so that he could not see. He told Eli, 'I have just come from the battle line; I fled from it this very day.' Eli asked, 'What happened, my son?' The man who brought the news replied, 'Israel fled before the Philistines, and the army has suffered heavy losses. Also your two sons, Hophni and Phinehas, are dead, and the ark of God has been captured.' When he mentioned the ark of God, Eli fell backward off his chair by the side of the gate. His neck was broken and he died, for he was an old man and heavy. He had led Israel forty years. His daughter-in-law, the wife of Phinehas, was pregnant and near the time of delivery. When she heard the news that the ark of God had been captured and that her father-in-law and her husband were dead, she went into labor [sic] and gave birth, but was overcome by her labor pains. As she was dying, the women attending her said, 'Don't despair; you have given birth to a son.' But she did not respond or pay any attention. She named the boy Ichabod, saying, 'The glory has departed from Israel'-because of the capture of the ark of God and the deaths of her father-in-law and her husband. She said, 'The glory has departed from Israel, for the ark of God has been captured'" (1 Sam. 4:12-22, NIV). When we share news about divine interventions in our lives, at times we are caught off guard and we seldom know how to respond. Some individuals employ defence mechanisms such as intellectualisation and rationalisation. Individuals who have not been tracking the divine guidance in our lives can be our worst enemies. They tend to be the hindrance to our progress. How do we handle the threats and the tauntings from individuals who learn about the new direction our lives are taking? It takes spiritual strength. It requires motivation, inspiration and inner zeal from the God of Heaven to move us beyond the harsh comments that we may endure. Negativity is poisonous. It eats away at our passion for God and the loudest call from Heaven can fall on deaf ears.

But God cares. He desires us to succeed and to be the best that we can be. It is through His insights and foreknowledge that we are propelled into becoming the spiritual vessel that He can work through. It's by being in contact with God that we respond affirmatively to His call on our lives.

Taking Time for Reflection [Jot down your thoughts]

- How do you think you would respond if you were to share the news about the changes you have made in your life?

- How settled are you in your mind about the changes that you have been or are planning to make?

- Are there any personal issues that you were confronted with as you read this chapter?

- How have you been reacting to your friends or acquaintances' views of your change of plans?

11
The Secret of My Victory

"Brokenness is a prerequisite to understanding God's grace, but the Christian Gospel does not leave us in a state of broken despair." (McMinn, *Psychology, Theology and Spirituality in Christian Counseling,* 1996:36)

At some point in our lives, we encounter problems that we seem not to have the ready solution. There are marital problems, parental problems, medical problems and I could go on. McMinn observes that "after trying for many weeks or months to cope without counselling, the potential client finally sets an appointment…."[37] When I reflected on my experiences up to this phase, it never dawned on me that I should have counselling for my financial problems. More strikingly, although I am trained in educational psychology up to postgraduate level, this did not even flash through my mind. In fact, I did not have a financial problem. That was the symptom of a spiritual issue which was the lack of spiritual insight. This means that spiritual problems predominantly require spiritual solutions. Here is where we bring the Christian God, Christ, and the Holy Spirit on board to share our fears and concerns in a practical and real way.

My condition undoubtedly warranted some long sessions of sustained and focused therapy until the solutions emerge. I was ignorant of this resource. Perhaps, it was for my good.

Being a Christian, I used the only resources that I was familiar with and which were inexpensive but invaluable. The numerous prayer and fast sessions I engaged in for the six months of my painful ordeal was my first term of reference. I wanted to know what was going on in my life and where 'I had lost control'. I was immersed in spiritual grief. Dejection and gloominess were etched over my strained face. The hour of prayer was a joy for me in the midst of hardship because it was a time when I pour my heart out to God. McMinn aptly depicts the need by contending that "when we pray, we humble ourselves and ask to become a partner in knowing and doing God's will."[38] It's a theological perspective that I subscribe to as my actions did reveal.

The Scripture reminds us to "pray without ceasing" (2 Thess.5:18). It is this type of spiritual activity that became my healing balm. Persistent prayer was necessary because I was trapped. I need to know why God was allowing the catalogue of catastrophic events to occur in my life. There was a passion within me to share my deep inner feelings with God. Great displeasure filled my heart immensely. I could not understand why circumstances and fortunes in my life had taken a turn for the worst. I held on to the biblical text "...that men ought always to pray and not to faint" (Lk. 18:1) How could I afford to bury my head in the sand. Although it was true that my predicament undeniably was bleak, it was not the time for apathy or hopelessness. I never knew defeat because my previous experiences as a young Christian demonstrated to me that "...we are more than conquerors through him that loved us" (Rom.8:37).

It was in my room during my prayer sessions that my inner self was exposed. I saw my sinful behaviour and I had to face up to it. The sessions were two-fold in that at first they uncovered my cloaked sins, caused me to see the need for repentance and also brought on a time of brokenness. I was stripped naked "For the eyes of the Lord range throughout the earth to strengthen those whose hearts are fully committed to him," 2 Chron. 16:9, NIV). At times I cried bitterly. My harsh conditions felt as though it was more than I could bear. Secondly, during those sessions I found healing from my putrefying spiritual wounds. It seemed as though I had to undergo the lacerations, the bruises, and experience the penetrating incisions. Prayer changes one's atmosphere. It provides an environment conducive to victory and living the Christian life. E White, in commenting on the significance of prayer, concludes that "Prayer is the opening of the heart to God as to a friend. Not that it is necessary in order to make known to God what we are, but in order to enable us to receive Him. Prayer does not bring God down to us, but brings us up to Him."[39] The moments of prayer provided comfort and relief. I felt a calm and peaceful atmosphere at the end of my prayer sessions. It was as if Christ had wrapped His loving and tender arms around me during the prayer sessions.

There were silent times and quiet moments when I would hum a song as I listened for what the Spirit wanted to say to me. As I went about my daily chores, I often sensed that the Lord wanted to say something to me. It was these types of realisations that urged me to be silent during some of my prayer sessions. This type of activity is biblical as we see with Jehosophat in 2 Chronicles 20 where the Lord instructed him to "set yourselves, stand ye still, and see the salvation of the Lord with you..." (verse 17). The Psalmist also experienced similar divine instructions: "Be still and know that I am God..." (Ps. 46:10).

Why did I have to engage in such intense prayer sessions? It's in the stillness of the moment and the serenity of the atmosphere that we hear God's voice distinctly. "Petitionary prayer creates in us a longing for God's will." [40] This was my spiritual state in that I had reached a point in my life where I needed direction and guidance. Specifically, I needed to know why the Lord allowed this travesty in my life. My heart was reaching out to learn God's purpose for my life. In Psalm 42:2 which says "My soul thirsteth for the living God…" I saw myself and truly felt my real need. That's why we must reach a point where we recognise that "to pray meaningfully, we must understand our deep thirst for God."[41] Ultimately, during our ordeals we must acknowledge "…that prayer is an important element of spiritual and psychological health. Prayer is at the heart of Christian piety, allowing us to humble ourselves…and to bring our concerns directly to God." [42]

Fasting is another powerful spiritual discipline that I used as I sought for answers. I longed for such sessions more and more, even though they were physically taxing and demanding. Food did not matter and neither were my studies at the time a priority. The material things of life become insignificant and useless when we are in dire trouble. No amount of academic achievements or material wealth will help us when our lives are in shambles.

From a biblical perspective, I saw the power in fasting. It adds to your prayer life in that it aids you in being focused on God. It is an overtly religious action employed by many who need to see the Mighty Hand of God working in their lives. Like David, when we are discontented with our circumstances and desperate, we will couple our prayer with fasting. That is why he "fasted, and went in, and lay all night upon the earth" (2 Sam. 12:16). Jehosophat would not rest nor eat until God responded and when we reach a spiritual low like Elijah, we too will desire to be in touch with God and move "…in the strength of that meal..." (1 Kings 19:8). Those like Queen Esther will refuse to see danger and ignore it. For such persons severe situations require drastic actions, hence, our resolve would be to "...fast ye for me, and neither eat nor drink three days, night nor day: I also and my maidens will fast likewise... and if I perish, I perish" (Esther 4:16). It is within this kind of atmosphere that we come close to God as we communicate with him and feel his almighty presence.

The other spiritual discipline I engaged in was intense and systematic bible studies. I searched the Scripture to see which biblical characters were in a similar situation to mine. Additionally, the Holy Spirit spoke to me directly from various biblical texts. I meditated on them moment by moment and I gained valuable and insightful counsel from the Word of God. It was "a lamp unto my feel and a light unto my path." (Ps. 119:105). What is fascinating is that the Psalmist was right when he posed the question: "Wherewithal shall a young man cleanse his way? By taking heed thereto according to thy word" (Ps. 119:9).

Although my friends and family were close by, praying with and for me, and giving support, it was the Scripture that redirected me. I drew closer to God and discovered that he was truly my Father because he spoke to me, guided me and showed me that I was going in the wrong direction. More importantly, the Word of God gave me inner strength and helped me developed greater faith in God. As I studied the Scripture, I discovered many promises that I held onto. They propelled me to keep trusting in God and to be bold as I walk through my 'valley of death'. As I have mentioned in chapter 5, I discovered mega-principles that helped to order my life. The bible became my map for travelling on this journey that God allowed me to take. I am grateful for these resources that are therapeutic in their own right. They did for me what a number of sessions in a counsellor's office may have done. I found great comfort by studying the Scripture. It was more than the studying. I mentally decided to apply the principles to my life and allow the Holy Spirit to work in me. My victory did not evolve or find its way by means of the usual process. Transformation and victory in one's life are the products of theological application of God's word. As Christians, it is to such resources that we need to turn, but we must know how to use them, lest they become tools to our hurt.

Taking Time for Reflection [Jot down your thoughts]

- How have you handled a devastating situation that occurred in your life?

- What feelings went through your mind? Were you feeling hopeless, unwanted?

- Think for a moment about the resources that you have used in the past during trying circumstances. Have they provided you with long-lasting hope and spiritual comfort?

- Which of the resources in this chapter have you ever thought of using in your personal experiences?

- How effective do you think they will be for your circumstances?

- Based on your situation, which of these would be prominent in helping you with your present situation?

12
Mission Accomplished!

"For he will finish the work and cut it short in righteousness: because a short work will the Lord make upon the earth." (Rom.9.28, KJV)

Mission Accomplished' is a phrase used in military circles to indicate the completion of a mission, particularly, combat operations. It was the same phrase that a USA President used to signal that a major military combat operation had ended. Such a phrase attempts to give a psychological boost to participants in a war or struggle. In using such a phrase, leaders seek to honour the heroic efforts of service persons, and they express their heart-felt gratitude for the risk of lives. This popular military language is suitable for individuals who have a need for achievement. It gives them mental superiority and demonstrates that they are worthy of their rewards.

Jesus' disciples had a glimpse and a foretaste of missionary work when they accompanied Him on His many journeys to Palestinian villages, towns and cities. They also got first-hand experience by witnessing and also performing numerous miracles such as raising dead people and healing blind people. Luke, the Third Evangelist, writing in his Gospel, relates Jesus' transaction with His twelve disciples by noting that when He "had called the Twelve together, he gave them power and authority to drive out all demons and to cure diseases, and he sent them out to preach the Kingdom of God and to heal the sick" (Lk 9.1-2, NIV). This enabled them to visit the Palestinian territories on their own, while being empowered to carry out their ministry. The author of the Third Gospel further recounts Jesus' command to seventy other followers "Go! I am sending you out like lambs among wolves" (Lk 10.3, NIV). These Gospel emissaries were ecstatic at the end of their mission, to the point that they "returned with joy and said, 'Lord, even the demons submit to us in your name'"(Lk 10.17,NIV). Certainly, this was a case of mission accomplished for these followers. Achieving a difficult task, especially in the midst of Satanic opposition, elicits inner zeal, propels us to move on, and creates a thirst to accomplish bigger missions. In fact, we tend to experience a sense of self-actualisation, knowing that we have achieved something beyond our capacity.

As time elapsed and having being instructed of what they should do, they began to get in motion. In deed, their mission was to be conducted throughout the entire world at that time (Acts 1.8). As a result, the Apostles and other followers responded to the missionary call and waited on Jesus to empower them for the task. The evidence of their empowered lives was seen in the way they cared for the poor and needy (Acts 6.1-4), healed the sick (Acts 3.1-8), and preached the Gospel. Did they complete the mission after Jesus had left? How did the persecutions and social unrest of that era impact on the execution of the mission?

In light of the different forms of deaths the disciples experienced, it seems that the mission was unfinished. Some of the disciples were beheaded, crucified upside down and others were stoned to death, all of which seemed to prevent them from closing their mission. From these gruelling experiences, it would seem that the Apostles could have carried on for a longer time. But, our heavenly Father knows best. He sees far beyond our myopic view and he thinks higher than our finite minds can comprehend. It was in His hands to allow these trials and difficulties to come their way.

The fact that Stephen was stoned to death while preaching (Acts 7) and James was beheaded (Acts 12.2) suggests that the builders and pillars of the Early Church were cut down in the line of duty. This was perceived as a means of hindering the mission from being accomplished. Although the first Apostles were driven off the scene, "...the church grew. New workers took the place of those who fell and stone after stone was added to the building."[43] The psychological warfare that the disciples had been struggling with had now resurfaced, with the Almighty One leading. This seemed to have plagued Herod who had planned to kill Peter, the angelic-delivered Apostle (Acts 12.3-17).

Did I finish the mission in which I was involved? I believe that the numerous complications in my life, the painful moments, the agonising experiences and the spiritual and emotional wounds that I suffered were there to strengthen and refine me for a greater purpose. My initial response during the early stage of my journey was that I would stay until the mission was completed. As I had stated earlier, I did not have a time limit on when I would complete my task, since such a mission tended to be ongoing. Being a youth mentor is tiring and involves going 'back and forth', particularly when young people vacillate between decisions and divine guidance. It is daunting, trying to provide spiritual guidance. One thing is certain. The Lord can and does work speedily, particularly in relation to the salvation of souls. The task need not be drawn out and painstaking. For me, the task of working with the young people had seemed to be a long one, in that it would involve a rebuilding process where there would be the need for a revived devotional life, inspiration, motivation, and commitment to the Lord.

Nevertheless, the intensity of our efforts through all-night prayer meetings, prayer and fast sessions, bible studies and other spiritual activities along with the power of the Holy Spirit, quickly brought about a high level of spirituality. I saw a revived group of young people who were willing to reach out to God and be what He wanted them to be. They could stand on their own through God's grace without the need to be mentored. The preparatory work had been completed, spiritual growth was taking place and maturity had been accomplished. This group of young people was active and I could see a huge difference now as opposed to some two years prior to this time.

We cut out the non-essentials, re-arranged our lives and searched for God's purpose in our lives. The things we refused to surrender, the Lord, in his love, ripped them from underneath us. Many times we cried and agonized because of our spiritual state. In it all, the Lord brought about the needed revival individually and corporately. As time went by, a structured and consistent monthly prison ministry was established in the nearby prison. This type of activity reinforces White's inspired thought that "Every son and daughter of God is called to be a missionary; we are called to the service of God and our fellowmen..."[44]

I continued to support and encourage everyone and assist my 'family' who, by this time, was experiencing a time of mourning. It was during the summer of 2001. Dad had just passed away. I also felt the pain of grief and agony. It was during this traumatic period that I felt I had accomplished the mission for which the Lord had brought me to the United Kingdom. I was even more pensive during this time. Deep on the inside, I felt the need to return to the Caribbean, however, I did not have the financial means to do so. Within my mind I was ready to go. There was that sense of satisfaction that I had done what the Lord really wanted me to do at that time. In my mind I was saying *It's time to go back home, I don't think I am needed here anymore and I would like to go now, if I could.* A few weeks after the funeral, I shared my inner thoughts with mum.

"I am thinking of going home," I said quietly.

"Don't say that. You just gave me an instant headache," she responded.

I felt it. I didn't mean to be insensitive to her ongoing grief at that time. We were both experiencing sorrow and this was the height of it for both of us. It was in the peak of the summer when I was still experiencing the impact from the bankruptcy. Mum had just laid dad to rest. It was very fresh in her psyche.

"Why do you want to go?" she queried.

"I just feel that it is time for me to pack up and go," I said rather dejectedly.

"And what about your studies? You haven't finished," she reminded me.

The studies at this time did not really matter. By this time, they were on the back-burner. In spite of the wrestling, I was at peace on the inside. I could not escape the awesome responsibility that the Lord had placed on my shoulders.

I had reached the pinnacle of this mountainous challenge and I sensed the need to let go. It was the climax of my trip to the United Kingdom and my journey through the dark night.

The waters were overflowing, they rose higher and higher, but they never swept me away. My bitter-sweet experiences impacted on my character and personality. I wasn't sure what would happen after this, even though I had a plan in my mind. These moments bring the joy that we long for in our hearts. They signal that we have stuck to the task.

More importantly, I believed that the Lord had been preparing me for this return trip. Although my departure from the UK sparked moments of agony and sadness for many, I did not have a choice. The Lord did not need me any longer in this part of the mission field (so I thought). I discovered that this was not quite true four years later. Nevertheless, it was the end of my missionary assignment and like the Apostle Paul, I can safely say that, "I have fought a good fight and I have finished my course. I have kept the faith" (2 Tim.4.7). The battle was gruelling, hard and painstaking. I was deeply wounded and, like Jacob, the Israelite Patriarch, I was limping. But in military language, I can safely say, 'Mission Accomplished!'

Taking Time for Reflection [Jot down your thoughts]

- Have you come to that place in your life where you can say that you have accomplished changes in your live?

- How would you describe the journey towards accomplishing your desire for a change?

- If you were to identify one thing that you would like to accomplish, having read this book, what would it be?

- How do you feel at this moment about all that is happening in your life?

- What is there in your life that you feel free in sharing with someone?

- How has the reading of this book helped you?

PART TWO
Applying Knowledge to Your Circumstances

13
Five Essential Principles for
Decision Making

"A Wise man is strong, yes, a man of knowledge increases strength"
(Prov. 24:5, NKJV)

While travelling on my journey, I was unaware of any useful principles or guidelines for the most part of this eventful experience. It was when I became stuck in my tracks and did not know how to escape that I turned to the Scripture. It was there that I found many principles that were instrumental in helping me make the decisions that I have subsequently come to make since then. A slow trek through the night-screening season is never smooth sailing and certainly is never palatable to the average human being. On the contrary, they are riddled with headaches, emotional pain and discouragement which could lead to depression, psychiatric illness or even physical death. However, having discovered these principles, I not only read and studied them, but realised that if I was going to succeed, I needed to apply them to my life.

During my extensive bible studies, I came across the following principles:

- Adverse situations during the divine leading in your life requires vindication of God's plan (Mosaic)

- Look on God and not on your multitude (Jehosophat)
- Lay the threats at the altar (Hezekiah)
- Wait for your mulberry tree top to shake (Davidian)
- Confirmation consolidates divine guidance (Gideonite)

In the many narratives surrounding each of these characters there is a unique experience from which I drew strength, comfort, and wisdom. It was from these experiences that I grasped the powerful principles which have been effective in helping me emotionally and spiritually. In examining the Mosaic principle, it is worth remembering that the inhabitants of Israel were practising idol worship with a golden calf while their leader, Moses, was in God's presence in Mount Sinai (Ex 32:1-6). It was this violation of the first Commandment that triggered God' intense fury to the extent that he was about to "consume them: and...make of thee a great nation (Ex. 32:10), he replied to Moses. Divine punishment was about to rain profusely on these erring helpless individuals. But this brave, insightful and visionary leader challenged the God of heaven by posing a heart-searching question: "why does your wrath burn hot against your people, whom you have brought out of the land of Egypt with great power and with a mighty hand?" (Ex. 32:11, NJKV). The principle is contained in Moses' plea "Why should the Egyptians speak, and say, 'He brought them out to harm them, to kill them in the mountain, and to consume them from the face of the earth'? Turn from Your fierce wrath, and relent from this harm to Your people" (Ex. 32:11, NKJV). Moses was pleading with God not to destroy the Israelites because the Egyptians would ridicule them about their God. The Israelite leader's eyes were open to the probability that this ungodly nation would be of the view that God intended to annihilate his people by bringing them into the wilderness.

In applying the principle, *adverse situations during the divine leading in your life requires vindication of God's plan for us,* put yourself in the Israelites' shoes and intercede for divine intervention in your life. The perspective we need to have is that if God does not deliver us from this difficult situation, then the ungodly who are around us will begin to taunt us with harsh criticisms such as, 'I know he/she was not really a Christian. He/she probably committed some terrible sin. God could never be leading him/her.' Such profound comments are debilitating and discouraging to any individual. This probable backlash causes us to ask for God's intervention, while we point out to Him the possible consequences. In focusing on Moses' plea, it is God's name that is at stake and is being ridiculed. The intercession, therefore, is focused on asking the God of heaven to demonstrate that he is leading us, in spite of our dire circumstances and difficult situations. The plea foreshadows the psalmist's sentiments "Why do the nations rage, and the people plot a vain thing? The kings of the earth set themselves, and the rulers take counsel together against the Lord and against his anointed" (2:1-2, NKJV). You don't need to stay in your rut forever, but know that you can take the challenge to God.

Having discovered how the first principle works, it is critical that we become determined in our minds so that the second principle can be applied in our lives. The principle, *look on God and not on your multitude,* emerges in light of Jehosophat predicament of his country being surrounded by great multitudes of armies. This Judean King had a well-guarded country (2 Chron 17:2,13-19) and thousands of mighty, courageous soldiers. Although the military strength of this country seems capable of winning the battle, Jehosophat organised a prayer and fast session to find out from the God of heaven what he should do. Sometimes, the 'great multitude' makes us become afraid and forces us to our knees in prayer. Our resources are not always the wisest things to use in times of difficulties. In order to overcome your 'great multitude', the following are worthwhile steps:

- spend some time in prayer and fasting
- discuss the matter with God
- reason with him about his promises and his plan for your life.

By doing this, it helps you put your situation into perspective and allows you to pinpoint God's location in this situation.

As you reach out to God in prayer, recognise your weakness and inability to fight with your 'great multitude'. In spite of the large amount of resources that you may have, without God they will become grasshoppers in the land of giants and hence, become ineffective. Be willing to admit to God that you are overwhelmed by your circumstances as you ask for his guidance on how to handle or respond to your situation. Additionally, be willing to admit that you don't know which way to turn or where to start. There are times when we just don't know what to do because we are baffled by the situation at hand. We are outfoxed to the extent that we don't have a clue about what is happening to our lives. To whom do you turn? How do you overcome your 'great multitude? The principle exists in the climax of this passionate prayer, "for we have no power against this great multitude that is coming against us; nor do we know what to do, but our eyes are upon you" (2 Chron.20:12).

It is certainly true that however massive our 'great multitude may be:

- we need to trust in God
- we must be determined that we will not do anything in ourselves to solve our situation
- we should be spiritually observant to how God is leading us and how he is working in our life.
- be aware that the enemy is present, but leave the negative and the adverse conditions to God.
- focus on your goal of staying connected with God.
- by doing this, you will be looking to God and not on the multitude.

The third principle, *lay the threats at the altar,* consists of practical elements which expose your faith in the God of heaven. In applying this principle, we need to follow Hezekiah's pattern in faith and look to Jehovah to deliver us and guide us. It is worth studying 2 Kings 18 and 19 and identify any similarities between Hezekiah's situation and your own. By engaging in a study of these chapters, you become familiar with Hezekiah's case and so discover how God guided the leader of his people. While you 'soak yourself in the Word of God', ask yourself questions such as where do I fit into this episode? How is my case similar? And what is God trying to say to me? As a parallel to Hezekiah receiving a letter from Rabshakeh,[45] a messenger in the Assyrian court (2 Kgs 19:14), we too may have received a threatening letter or we can write out our situation or request, which now becomes a 'document'.

It is at this stage that our faith becomes tested even more as we do the following:

- Go into the house of the Lord or in your normal prayer room with the letter or written 'document'.
- Literally spread the letter or your written 'document' with your case before the Lord.

- Intercede on behalf of your situation.
- Wait for the Lord to respond to your intercessory prayer.

In applying this principle, note that God works at his own pace and in his own time, hence we need to give God space to work his will out in our lives as opposed to looking for positive answers now. Additionally, there should be the determination in our hearts that we will wait for God to deliver us.

'Wait for your mulberry tree top to shake' is a principle which has emerged from a series of intercessory prayers. On reflecting on King David's attitude in terms of decision-making, we encounter a passionate leader who needed specific answers to specific questions which were made during specific prayer requests. Each time he was about to attack the Philistines nation, he asked for divine direction and guidance (1 Sam. 23:2, 4-13; 30:7-8; 2 Sam. 5:18-20). It was a case of heeding the instructions of the wisdom seen in Proverbs 3 verse 6, "In all thy ways acknowledge him and he will direct your path." More importantly, we need to ask ourselves the question, "How willing am I to allow the God of heaven to direct my life and to determine what happens in my 'world?' David's asking for God's guidance underpins the desire to establish a relationship with Jehovah. This demonstrates the need for us, as individuals, also to develop a relationship with God. Such a relationship is what placed this mighty leader in a position to hear God's instructions concerning the tree-top noise.

David was at a critical stage in his pursuit of and battle with the Philistines when he specifically asked the God of heaven if he should attack this nation. As I examined the divine reply (2 Sam. 5:23-24), I noticed an unusual pattern in that David was directed to

- wait for God's signal
- watch for the specific sign that God had given
- be willing to respond urgently.

In applying this principle, it is important that you involve God in your plans through prayer and ask him to show you what would be your 'mulberry tree'. In every situation, there is a 'mulberry tree' that God wants to shake to alert us that he is leading us. The mulberry tree signals to us that it's time to move on because God has now given us the requested victory. What could be your 'mulberry tree'? Is there a situation that you can present to God asking him to intervene in a particular way according to his will? Be willing and be determined to follow God's leading in your life as you present your case(s) to him. One thing is crucial: however loud the mulberry tree top shakes, be willing to respond obediently.

When we are caught between two decisions and we just don't know which way to turn, we are not sure that it is the God of heaven who is leading us along a particular path, it is helpful to ask for confirmation. Gideon found himself in a similar position which led him to ask God for some signs. Here the principle, *confrontation consolidates divine guidance* emerges as God provides signs for Gideon. Did Gideon doubt God? What was it about Gideon that he so desperately needed signs? When we take Gideon's socio-economic status into consideration, we realise that he was the least of all people who should be selected to deliver God's people from the enemy. By his own admission, his "clan is the weakest…" and he is "the least in his father's house" (Judges 6:15, NKJV). Isn't it a wonder that God often uses the 'misfits' of society and the have-nots? For Gideon, this call from God, this divine commission could not be real, hence Gideon needed confirmation. A sign would be vital in advancing on this mission. We should never underestimate God because his nature leads him to perform unpopular deeds. But, while such may seem to be foolishness, to God it is wisdom. It is principles like these that guide us and help us to find hope in the Word of God.

Taking Time for Reflection [Jot down your thoughts]

- What critical decisions are facing you at this time?

- Which of these principles can you apply to each of these decisions?

- How willing are you to engage in any of the three major spiritual resources (fasting, prayer, intensive bible study)that you have encountered in this book?

- Identify three (3) lessons you have learnt from reading this chapter.

- What type of sacrifices will you have to make in applying these principles to your situations?

- The divine clock ticks at a different speed to ours. In light of this view, how willing are you prepared to wait on the God of heaven for a response to your circumstances?

- Having read the book, what new things have you encountered?

- How would you compare your spiritual situation now as opposed to when you began reading this book

EPILOGUE
The Hand of God

Almost every time natural disasters such as floods, hurricanes, and tsunamis strike, they rob us of life, comfortable surroundings, and material possessions. The initial reaction to such devastating events is always expressed in the words 'acts of God'. As human beings, we seem not to have an explanation for such phenomena and so we look to heaven for the answer. But, this is more to cast aspirations on the Christian God than to seek for answers. Why would human beings, in spite of our religious persuasions attribute these natural occurrences to this deity? Is there a deeper longing and searching in the pre-conscious portion of the mind for the unexplainable to be answered? Are there struggles concerning the sovereignty of this deity in cosmic affairs and anthropological destiny?

Newspaper headlines, television, and radio top-stories tend to court our emotions, play with the unconscious part of the mind in an attempt to place the blame squarely at the feet of God. BBC News carried an article online entitled Acts *of God?* in which the following question was asked: "How could a God, or some other force for good, have orchestrated a natural disaster with such dreadful consequences?"[46] Immediately, we tend to reach out and agree, if not vocally, mentally. It's the type of response that is inevitable, because there seems to be no alternative.

The effects of Hurricane Katrina on New Orleans is seen as an "act of God" that destroyed a city. But our feelings about and perceptions of events are stored in the unconscious part and cannot rise to the surface easily.[47] They are silently shaping our potential responses. No wonder we encounter battles between the divine and human wills. The presence of these views impacts on our experiences and lives. With the mind being tuned into these headlines, our thoughts are channelled in that direction. In taking a closer look at the phrase 'Act of God', I noticed its similarity to the 'Hand of God', hence the reason for the title of the epilogue.

The expression, 'Hand of God' features in the lives of many biblical characters such as Ezra and Nehemiah. It was a big issue for countries such as ancient Israel and the surrounding nations such as Ashdod (1 Sam. 5:6, 9,11). These individuals and inhabitants experienced what the 'Hand of God' felt like. At times, they were surprised by God's intervention. Other times, they were gradually encouraged to be part of a wider plan for the inhabitants and other ethnic groups. We note every time the 'Hand of God' moved upon someone's life, dramatic changes occurred for good or bad. But the moving Hand of God expects obedience, surrender, and submission. Our human wills become harder to achieve and our eagerness to get on with our personal lives is thwarted because of the shift in perspectives that comes when God moves in our lives.

But what does the 'Hand of God' feel like? Does it have two sides similar to our natural hand? Does it affect those on whom it rest? Manfred Dreytza commented on the Hebrew word [yad] in referring specifically to the Lord by saying that it is used metaphorically to illustrate Israel's first hand experience of divine deliverance from Egyptian torture.[48] How has the 'Hand of God' moved upon the people's lives? Biblical evidence reveals the providential manoeuvring of Yahweh, thus leading to special favours and blessings (Ezra 7:6; 8:18, 22; Neh.2:8, 18).

Passionate leaders like Ezra had been faced with pressure from government sources (Ezra 5:3) which attempted to circumvent the restoration work on the Israelites' temple. These are the types of circumstances which we face as we undertake our spiritual journeys. When our lives are riddled with difficulties and spiritual obstacles, we are forces to "... seek the Lord of Israel..." (Ezra 6:22). We ascribe our success and our spiritual victories to the Christian God who prompts human beings to aid us. And as Ezra stood between earthly authorities and the exiled Israelites, "...the King granted him all his request, according to the hand of the Lord his God upon him" (Ezra 7:6).

This hand is seen as that mighty prevailing power that permeates the lives of individuals to ensure success, protection and progress. On the other hand, judgement is another display of the 'Hand of God'. In this case, it is a punishing hand weighing heavily on individuals. For Ezra points out that "the hand of our God is upon all them for good that seek him; but his power and his wrath is against all them that forsake him" (8.22). Moreover, Samuel understood the devastation that nations can experience. It can bring about total annihilation where he stated that "...the hand of the Lord was heavy upon them of Ashdod, and he destroyed them..." (1 Sam.5:6). Here we encounter the two-fold 'Hand of God' ensuring equality, justice and ultimately salvation. The two sides seem equally powerful. Whether it is a salvation experience or punitive act, we feel the impact, recognise the effect and must therefore, submit to the almighty power that exists. Escaping from the 'Hand of God' is improbable. How few have felt its weight and escaped? How free is our conscience? This hand overshadows us at every turn and we are guided in seeing the love for every individual as Yahweh seeks to lay His gracious hands on us.

Experiencing the Hand of God leads to a time of reflection so that we may come to grips with our own inner emotions and thoughts. Where is it leading us? Are we prepared for the path ahead? Will we fight against this Hand so that our agenda become the primary aim? It brings us face to face with the challenges in our lives and instigates an honest response to the divine promptings. How we perceive the touch from this Hand determines the journey we undertake. Within the recesses of our hearts we experience pain. We face up to challenges and are broken by this Hand. We can be comforted in the thought that the Hand of God strengthens the weak, empowers the struggling and protects the vulnerable. Ultimately, we must admit that all our hopes and achievement, all our spiritual developments were "according to the good hand of my God upon me" (Neh. 2:8).

Taking Time for Reflection [Jot down your thoughts]

- To whom do you attribute the devastating or successful events in your life?

- What thoughts arise deep in the sub-conscious part of your mind as you reflect on your situation?

- Does the Hand of God move over your life for good or as punishment?

- What is your perspective of your situation now that you have read this book?

- Have there been any 'natural disasters' in your life? What message do you think they have been trying to send to you?

- Has it been possible for you to come up with an explanation for some or all of these 'natural disasters' which occurred in your life? What reasons can you give?

APPENDIX
Spiritual Guidance for Personal Devotions

More often than not, we tend to encounter difficulties in engaging in personal devotions. Without a routine, we become stuck, overpowered, and overwhelmed by a million and one chores around us. In the end we simply don't know how to escape. We find it challenging to rise in the morning or to stay up late at night to spend quality time with our Saviour and Redeemer.

Having read the entire book, you may be wondering how you can begin to apply some of this stuff in your life. Here are a few ideas that can get you started. Apart from the usual way in which most people pray, we need to be cognisant of the fact that we will never move beyond the normal way of praying until we ask God to give us the Spirit of prayer. This is based on the events in the book of Acts where we encounter the disciples travelling to the temple at prayer time to attend a prayer session (Acts 3.1). Interestingly, this was their pattern. Luke reminds us that "Every day they continued to meet together in the temple courts" (Acts 2.46, NIV).

Additionally, the Apostle Paul reminded the Ephesian Christians to "pray in the Spirit on all occasions with all kinds of prayers and requests. With this in mind, be alert and always keep on praying for all the saints" (Eph 6.18, NIV). How do we keep praying for each other? How can we engage in intercessory prayer, supplicatory prayer, thanksgiving prayer and prayer of praise if the Holy Spirit does not give us such a desire, zeal or inspiration to prayer?

As you prepare to embark on this journey of engaging in personal devotions, ask the Lord to wake you up early (possibly an hour before you prepare for work or school)or keep you up late at night. With that in mind, I share the following:

- Identify a Christian book to read. It should be one that meets your needs, depending on where you are spiritually. **You can jot do any thoughts or ideas that were beneficial to you.**

- Provide yourself with a prayer journal (a small book) and jot down the issues that you would like to present to God. If the list is too long, you can divide the items into groups as follows:

Sunday
Job
children
Relatives

Monday
friends
studies

Tuesday
Church activities

Wednesday
husband/wife
My spiritual your church post

By doing this you would be able to pray for something different everyday. By the end of the week, you would have interceded for all the things on your list.

- Spend a few minutes worshipping the Creator in singing songs, hymns or choruses.

- Take some time for prayer, focusing on the needs in your prayer list. However, allow the Holy Spirit to guide as to what you should be praying about (**Check Rom 8.26**).

- Spend a few minutes in quiet reflection, meditating on a bible text or song.

- Based on what transpired during your prayer session and reflection time, ask the Holy Spirit to speak to you. Allow the Lord to guide you to His word.

- Read and study that portion of Scripture and write down any insights you gain from reading/studying the texts.

By following this routine consistently, and earnestly praying about your spiritual life, you can be helped in your personal devotions and by extension, in spiritual life.

As you progress, you could find that you need more time than you are giving to this aspect of your life. You can decide to spend longer time during this phase or have another session during the day or night. It's important to develop the routine and to maintain it by disciplining yourself. More importantly, it's about asking the Holy Spirit to wake you up on time to spend time in prayer so that you may draw closer to the God of Heaven.

NOTES

[1] Jo Ann Davidson, 'The God Who Calls Again' in *Adventist Review,* IAD edn., May, 1998, p. 8-13 (8).

[2]Ellen G. White, *Christ's Object Lesson* (Washington, D.C.: Ellen G. White Pubs., 1923), p.374.

[3] ___________ *Keys to Happiness* (Maryland: Review & Herald, 2000), p. 40.

[4] John Youngberg & Millie Youngberg, *Rebuilding the Family Altar: Meeting the End-time Challenges* (Florida: IAD, 1994), p. 60.

[5] Ellen G. White, *Ministry of Healing* (Nampa, ID: Pacific Press, 1942), p.58.

[6] John T. Squires, 'Acts' in James D. G. Dunn and John W. Rogerson (eds.), Eerdmans Commentary on the Bible (Grand Rapids, MI: William B. Eerdmans Publishing Co.,2003), pp 1213-1267 (1216).

[7] Charles S. Carver & Michael F. Scheier, *Perspectives on Personality*, 3rd ed., (Boston, MA: Allyn and Bacon, 1996), p.66.

[8] Squires, 'Acts' p. 1218.

[9] Richard J. Coggins, '1 and 2 Chronicles' in James D. G. Dunn and John W. Rogerson (eds.), Eerdmans Commentary on the Bible (Grand Rapids, MI: William B. Eerdmans Publishing Co.,2003), pp 282-312 (303).

[10] Youngberg &Youngberg, *Rebuilding the Family Altar*, p.53.

[11] Ibid., p.54.

[12] Ibid., p.56.

[13] Kenneth H. Maahs, *The John You Never Knew: Decoding the Fourth Gospel* (New York: Peter Lang Publishing, Inc., 2006), p. 163.

[14] Bruce Milne, *The Message of John* (Leicester, UK: Inter-Varsity Press, 1993), p.310.

[15] Ellen G. White, *Patriarchs and Prophets* (Mountain View, CA: Pacific Press Publishing Association, 1890), p.645.

[16] Ralph Tenthani, 'Madonna's adoption Divides Malawi' , *BBC News,*Lilongwe, October 16, 2006.

[17] White, *Patriarchs and Prophets*, p. 243.

[18] Child Welfare Information Gateway, 'Impact of Adoption on Adopted Persons: A Factsheet for Families' *http://www.childwelfare.gov/pubs/f adimpact.cfm* (2004) [Accessed January 31, 2006].

[19] Ellen G. White, *Acts of the Apostle,*(Mountain View, CA: Pacific Press, 1941), p.357.

[20] Mark R. McMinn, *Psychology, Theology and Spirituality in Christian Counseling,*(Wheaton, IL: Tyndale House Publishers, Inc., 1996), p.35.

[21] McMinn, *Psychology, Theology and Spirituality in Christian Counseling,* p.36.

[22] Davidson, 'The God Who Calls Again', p.10.

[23]Ellen G. White, *Messages to Young People* (Washington, D.C.: Ellen G. White Pubs., 1958), p.117.

[24] Davidson, 'The God Who Calls Again', p.10.

[25] Gary Collins, *Christian Counseling: A Comprehensive Guide, rev. edn.* (Dallas, TX: Word Publishing, 1988), p.93.

[26] Ibid.

[27] Patrick Young, 'Glaucoma and Neurodegeneration' http://www.rpbusa.org/library content (2004) [Accessed February 6, 2007].

[28] Philip J. Budd, 'Numbers' in J. Dunn and J. Rogerson (eds.), *Eerdmans Commentary on the Bible* (Grand Rapids, MI: William B. Eerdmans Publishing Company, 2003), pp.125-152 (148).

[29] Milne, *The Message of John,* p.315.

[30] Craig A. Evans, 'Mark' in J. Dunn and J. Rogerson (eds.), *Eerdmans Commentary on the Bible* (Grand Rapids, MI: William

B. Eerdmans Publishing Company, 2003), pp.1064-1103 (1068).

[31] Donna Partow, *Becoming a Vessel God Can Use*, (Minneapolis Minnesota: Bethany House Publishers, 1996), p.50.

[32] Ibid.

[33] Gary Collins, *Christian Counseling: A Comprehensive Guide, rev. edn.* (Dallas, TX: Word Publishing, 1988), p.93.

[34] Ibid., p.94.

[35] Collins, *Christian Counseling: A Comprehensive Guide,* p.93.

[36] Carver & Scheier, *Perspectives on Personality*, p.168.

[37] McMinn, *Psychology, Theology and Spirituality in Christian Counseling,* p.32.

[38] Ibid., p.71.

[39] Ellen G. White, *Steps to Christ*, (Mountain View, CA: Pacific Press, 1892), p.93.

[40] McMinn, *Psychology, Theology and Spirituality in Christian Counseling,* p.71.

[41] Ibid., p.75.

[42] Ibid., p. 76.

[43] Ellen G. White, *Acts of the Apostle*,(Mountain View, CA: Pacific Press, 1941), p.597.

[44] ____________________, *Ministry of Healing*, p.395.

[45] He was also the chief of the princes, the name given to the chief cup-bearer or the vizier of the Assyrian court. See 2 Kings 18:17-37 for the narration of the story. He and the other envoys returned to their master and reported that Hezekiah and his people would not submit.

[46] BBC News, *An Act of God? BBC News,* Jan.3, 2005.

[47] Carver & Scheier, *Perspectives on Personality*, p. 201.

[48] Manfred Dreytza, 'Yad' in Willen A. Van Gemeren (ed.), *New International Dictionary of Old Testament Theology and Exegesis Vol. 2* (Cumbria, UK: Paternoster Press, 1996), p. 403.

2853250

Made in the USA